forgive
eness

Paberback ISBN: 979-8-9867211-0-1
ePub ISBN: 979-8-9867211-1-8

Library of Congress Control Number (LCCN): 2023900365

Good Soil Press
St. Paul, Minnesota

Cover and interior design:
The Brand Office

MARK HENDERSON
MICHAEL SNUFFER

forgive
ness

A SURPRISING
WAY FORWARD

Good Soil Press

PART THREE
THE CASE FOR FORGIVENESS

PART FIVE
FORGIVENESS IN LIFE'S
TOUGHEST SITUATIONS

preface

AS YOU CAN SEE on the cover, this book is authored by two
people: Mark Henderson and Michael Snuffer. For well over a decade,
we have each worked with individuals and couples trying to find a
way forward in the middle of difficult circumstances. We find it very
fulfilling to dig into the hardest parts of life with individuals and
couples. God has equipped us with a powerful set of counseling tools
which bring healing to individuals and marriages. In 2012, we started
Equip2Counsel™ with our wives, a ministry which trains believers
around the world in these counseling tools.

As we travel and teach these principles to professional and lay
ministers, it is gratifying to see God's truth applied to these tools and
the most difficult circumstances. We feel like God has given us a front
row seat to miracles as lives are transformed, individuals experience
emotional healing, and broken relationships are rebuilt. We decided it
is time to record some of these principles and make the tools available

to a wider audience. As we prayerfully considered the subject matter for this book, one topic kept rising to the surface—*forgiveness.*

Forgiveness is a powerful resource God has given to his children. It brings healing to a wide range of difficult situations. While we apply many different tools in our counseling offices, forgiveness is one common component nearly every situation requires.

Forgiveness is one of the foundational principles of the Bible. Jesus' death on the cross established the basis for God's forgiveness. Those of us who have accepted Jesus Christ as our Lord and Savior have experienced this forgiveness and believe it allows us to live in an ongoing relationship with God.

Unforgiveness is an area where people often get stuck. Even men and women who are believers and grew up in the church often have trouble applying the biblical principles of forgiveness in a way which brings real freedom. As a result, many are unable to move beyond the hurts of the past.

As we wrote this book, we set out with one goal: to bring a more practical understanding of the biblical principles of forgiveness. We want to give readers a roadmap for practicing forgiveness so all may experience the healing and freedom God promises.

We have taught these principles to hundreds of individuals. This book is a response to many who asked, "Do you have this written down somewhere?" It is our hope that you will be able to clearly understand the biblical principles and practice the steps explained in this book. We pray you will experience the freedom and healing God gives when we practice forgiveness.

We, Mark and Michael, worked together from beginning to end on this book, but in order to eliminate confusion, it is written in the first person with one voice ("I" not "We"). It was gratifying to see how God brought our shared understanding of these principles to this final product. This co-authoring process resulted in a more helpful book than either of us could have authored independently!

There are many stories told in this book, drawn from the lives and ministries of both Mark and Michael. All are based on real events or meetings with real people, but in order to protect the identity of our clients, the names and certain identifying details have been changed.

We have met and worked with hundreds of people, some with fairly similar stories, which brings us to an important point. It's easy for *all* of us to feel like we are alone, that no one else in the whole world has faced this same situation. The reality is—we are not alone, and our circumstances are less unique than we may realize. "What has been will be again, what has been done will be done again; there is nothing new under the sun" (Ecclesiastes 1:9). It was even surprising to us how many stories could have been applied to multiple people and situations. So, to our friends and past clients, if you read a particular story and wonder whether it is about you…most likely we did *not* have you in mind.

We hope you enjoy reading this book as much as we have enjoyed writing it. Scripture teaches us that a knowledge of spiritual concepts— by itself—is not spiritual growth (1 Corinthians 8:1-2). Gaining an understanding is just the start. Spiritual growth occurs when it changes who we are and the way we do life (James 2:20-26). Our prayer is that you acquire a more complete understanding of forgiveness and experience real change and spiritual growth in your life through the practice of forgiveness.

PART ONE

UNLOCKING OUR
THINKING PATTERNS

1

how not why

MATT WAS HAVING the day of his life! Not only did the team win, but Matt personally intercepted two passes. In the locker room, Coach announced that Matt was the season's first defenseman named "Player of the Game." He felt so proud as Coach tossed him the game ball and teammates congratulated him.

Mom met Matt in the parking lot with a huge hug and an even bigger smile. Her voice was full of pride as she praised him for a great game and for the game ball tucked under his arm.

Dad was waiting in the car. Matt excitedly jumped in the back seat and recounted each big play. He proudly showed the game ball to his parents. His dad blurted out a quick, "That's great!" but then proceeded to tell his son all the things he did wrong in the game.

"You got beat on that play in the second quarter because you were too close to the line."

"You dropped that third interception because you took your eyes off the ball."

"You looked pretty sluggish in the fourth quarter."

Matt's body slumped back into his seat as the critique continued. His shoulders sank, and his smile faded away. Something inside him broke that night. Matt realized he would never measure up to his father's expectations.

Matt's dad was never around. When they did spend time together, his dad was very critical. As a young boy, Matt eagerly worked for his dad's approval, but in his teen years, Matt began to despise his father. He continued to get good grades and became a starter on the football team, but no matter what he accomplished, he was still criticized.

As Matt became more and more frustrated, he treated his father with disrespect. Matt often verbally lashed out at his dad. This, of course, made his father angry. Matt's dad retaliated by making cutting remarks. Even worse, he would turn away from Matt with a dismissive wave and walk off.

The feelings of hurt and anger Matt felt toward his father continued to grow. Although he stayed in touch with his family through college and into early adulthood, Matt's relationship with his dad remained shallow and distant.

After graduating from college, Matt found a good job and a girl he really liked. But Matt was struggling. He managed his anger pretty well in public, but his girlfriend and the people closest to him usually bore the brunt of it. Matt knew his anger was often irrational, and he didn't understand why stupid, little things infuriated him so much. His outbursts became frequent, and he avoided the people he cared about the most, especially his girlfriend.

Matt also suffered from insomnia. He lay awake late into the night with a sea of thoughts swimming around in his mind. Sometimes he had one more drink than he should—just to turn the thoughts off and be able to sleep. It wasn't unusual for Matt to start his workday feeling totally exhausted after a nearly sleepless night. During an annual checkup, he asked his doctor about some intermittent abdominal pains. The doctor said, "It's unusual to have stomach issues at your age." He recommended slight diet changes and warned Matt about the need to manage his stress levels.

Faith was part of Matt's life. He accepted Christ as his personal Savior in high school, but now, Jesus seemed more distant than ever. Matt knew God wanted a relationship with him, but when he prayed, he often wondered if God really cared or was listening to him. He wanted to feel closer to God but didn't know how. He came to this conclusion: *Maybe God doesn't want to be so personal in my life. Maybe God just expects me to go to church and be a good person.*

But then a new realization alarmed Matt. He was becoming the person he swore he would never become. Matt was becoming like his father. His anger caused him to make cutting, critical remarks, even though he knew this was hurting the people he cared for the most. He hated that he was so quick to point out faults. He hated that he had developed a critical spirit. Matt didn't want to hurt his friends, so he began to push everyone away. He was critical, angry, and distant.

Matt told his trusted friend, Tom, that he was struggling and thinking of breaking up with his girlfriend. Tom shared about relationship struggles of his own and the help he found through our counseling ministry at church. Tom knew Matt still deeply cared for his girlfriend and encouraged him to come and talk with me before he made such a final decision.

A NEW WAY OF THINKING

One of the foundational principles of our caring ministry, Equip-2Counsel™, is "How Not Why." It's a principle which guides the way we help people understand where they are stuck. This principle gives people a new and different way forward in many areas of life, including forgiveness. It is a baseline we see God use to make life-altering change and bring people lasting freedom.

What is the difference between "Why" and "How?" Isn't understanding "Why" more important? What does all this have to do with forgiveness?

JEANIE

Jeanie came into the office because she was sick and tired of being sick and tired. Her actions and life choices destroyed two marriages, and she struggled in her relationships with her kids. Her daughter was so tired of feeling hurt, she wouldn't talk to Jeanie anymore. This weighed heavily on her, and she carried with her a constant weight of shame and self-condemnation.

As we began to unpack her story, Jeanie shared with me how sex and drugs had been a part of her life since childhood. She told stories about her mother's many boyfriends and how these men mistreated her in abusive ways throughout her childhood and teen years.

Jeanie was aware of the detrimental impact these traumatic experiences had on her young mind. Even as a pre-teen, she became addicted to sex. By the age of seventeen, Jeanie had slept with dozens of boys and men. Jeanie started taking drugs to escape her pain and guilt. The drugs soon became an addiction. She also learned how skilled she was at manipulating people. To fund her addiction, she used these skills to deal drugs and run a profitable little "business."

Jeanie became a Christian in her late teen years and changed many of these behaviors. She stopped the drugs and sex and graduated from high school, but when things got difficult, she turned back to sex and drugs to escape reality. These behaviors took a huge toll on her relationships. She destroyed two marriages, and her children became resentful of her.

Jeanie was able to explain to me the reasons "why" she acted out in these ways. She clearly articulated the way her upbringing and childhood experiences led her down this path in life. She had a solid understanding of why she did all these things, but Jeanie was still stuck—and still hurting! Her knowledge of the reasons for her behavior did not motivate her to make better choices when life became difficult.

When things got rough for Jeanie, and the pain of life felt too great, recounting "the reasons why" reinforced a victim mentality. She could not change her past, so recounting all the reasons why she became addicted to drugs and sex made her feel like she was nothing more than a victim to her circumstances. This victim mentality fueled her addictions:

"The reason I act out in these ways is…"

"I don't really have a choice, because…"

But at the same time, knowing and believing these reasons did not stop the pounding waves of shame and self-condemnation Jeanie would feel after she would act out. She was tired of being stuck and wanted me to help her find another way.

We met and talked for our allotted time, but I didn't want Jeanie to leave without some real hope that change was possible. So, we decided to extend her appointment. As Jeanie began to explain another one of her reasons for her behavior, I interrupted her mid-sentence and said, "I think I understand enough about 'why' you do the things you do. I want to help you understand 'how' your brain takes you down this destructive path. I want to give you a new way to direct your thought patterns that can bring lasting change and freedom."

RENEWING YOUR MIND

In Romans 12:2, the Apostle Paul writes, "Do not conform to the pattern of this world, but be transformed by the renewing of your mind. Then you will be able to test and approve what God's will is—his good, pleasing and perfect will."

Many of us who have been in the church for some years are quite familiar with this passage. We have heard it quoted and preached on in many sermons. We have discussed it in small groups. Some have even memorized it. But perhaps there is more for us to learn from this passage.

Paul communicates the following truth about our minds in this passage: 1) God wants to work with us to renew our minds, and 2) God has given us the ability to renew our minds. This means God gives us the ability to create new patterns in our minds! These new patterns can bring about life change. They can transform the way we think and—as a result—transform the way we live!

God wants to help us renew our minds. We might believe it more easily for others than we do for ourselves. We believe God can transform broken lives into something beautiful. His grace has the power to bring change, and we praise God together when we see it in the lives of those around us. But don't we often feel powerless to bring about real change in our own lives? In my heart of hearts, do I believe I have the God-given power to transform my mind and to renew my thinking so completely that I am set free from old, unwanted patterns?

When individuals meet with me, I often ask, "Do you believe God has the power to bring life-changing freedom to everyone?"

Most immediately respond, "Yes, God has the power to bring freedom, and He loves everyone!"

Then when I ask, "Do you believe God can and will free you?"

I often get a tentative response, "Well… um… I guess… I… um…"

In my ministry, I walk through life issues with men and women who have stopped believing God gives *them* the ability to renew *their* minds. Many of these individuals are active in ministry. They serve or lead ministries where they see the transformational power of God in the lives of others, but they feel stuck and abandoned by God when it comes to experiencing positive spiritual change in their own lives.

It seems even the Apostle Paul had this experience at some point in his Christian walk. He talks about these feelings of hopelessness in extremely personal and emotional terms in chapter 7 of this same letter to the Romans. He writes,

> [21]…Although I want to do good, evil is right there with me. [22] For in my inner being I delight in God's law; [23] but I see another law at work in me, waging war against the law of my mind and making me a prisoner of the law of sin at work within me. [24] What a wretched man I am! Who will rescue me from this body that is subject to death? (Romans 7:21-24)

Doesn't Paul sound like his life is out of control? He's a wretched man who sets out to do the good things he knows God wants him to do but keeps getting pulled back into the sinful patterns of the world. He has a good spirit trapped in an evil man's flesh. At some time in his Christian life, Paul felt stuck. He felt like he had no ability to transform his own mind and life in any positive or lasting way.

But fortunately, Paul does not stop here. God gives us hope through the next words Paul writes: "[24]...Who will rescue me from this body that is subject to death? [25] Thanks be to God, who delivers me through Jesus Christ our Lord!" (Romans 7:24-25a)

Paul clearly related to feeling hopeless and helpless to change his own life, but he learned this important truth: God gives us the ability to change the patterns of thought in our brains in a way that transforms how we live.

And with this ability comes the *responsibility* to renew our minds. Jesus left the comfort of heaven and lived here for thirty-three years. He willingly gave himself up to his enemies and died an excruciating death. Why? He did it to give us the power to transform our minds and be set free from worldly patterns of thought which derail our choices and our lives. Since we have the ability, it is our responsibility to cooperate with God and complete the transformation of our minds, removing our old patterns and replacing these with godly thinking.

Jesus' death and resurrection give us both the ability and the responsibility to renew our minds. He will gladly walk alongside us and provide the wisdom needed to carry out this responsibility.

THE "WHY" DANGER

"I have a problem with rage because my parents constantly yelled at me."

"I had an affair because my wife does not meet my physical and emotional needs."

"I drink to escape the pain of my dysfunctional family."

"I don't want to be a workaholic, but I was raised in a family that never had enough."

Asking the "why" question can help us understand the reasons we struggle in certain areas of our lives. However, answers to the "why" question can bring false hope because the answers we receive do not lead us to freedom.

In fact, I often see the opposite is true. Dwelling on the reasons why can add power to sinful behaviors already trying to control us. The reasons are typically true, further reinforcing a victim mentality. Parents modeling bad behavior *is* a reason we learned this behavior. Unmet physical and emotional needs *do* cause us to want to look outside our marriage. Living in a dysfunctional home *is* painful and *can* motivate us to find unhealthy ways to medicate and escape the pain.

These truths end up reinforcing in our minds the lie that we have no choice. Though we know these behaviors are inappropriate or sinful, we feel like we are on autopilot and powerless to change.[1] Consequently, it leaves us feeling truly stuck!

In addition, we are powerless to change the reasons why. No one can change their parents or their upbringing. No one chooses the family they are born into, and it is not possible to heal all of one's dysfunctional relationships. A spouse cannot change whether their needs have been met in the past, and there is no guarantee their spouse will meet their needs in the future. The reasons are often true, and we are usually unable to fix them.

For example, a man may say, "Of course I lose my temper a

---

1   Larson, Dr. Al, *Theosynergistic Neuro-Transformation: Cooperating with God for a Change*, (Dynamics of Growth, 2003), p. 3.

lot. I'm Irish!" Are Irish people known to have a short temper? Do some Irish families model this trait and pass it down to the children? While both might be true, how does one change "being Irish?" It is impossible! When we only focus on the reasons why, we are in danger of inadvertently justifying and rationalizing inappropriate and destructive behaviors. Though it may be helpful to understand the reasons, this information—by itself—often adds power to the unhealthy behaviors. Bursts of willpower may allow us to white-knuckle our way through periods of temporary restraint, but true lasting change often feels further out of reach.

> when we only focus on the reasons why, we are in danger of inadvertently rationalizing unhealthy behaviors

This was true for Jeanie. She had no trouble understanding the reasons for her behaviors in the areas of sex and drug use. As you recall, she very clearly and adeptly self-diagnosed and then explained to me all the reasons. She experienced long periods when she, through sheer force of will, would successfully suppress these behaviors. But when things got hard, she was repeatedly drawn back to the old lifestyle as a way out.

God gives us the ability (and the responsibility) to renew our minds. Simply understanding the "why" is not enough to bring this renewal. In fact, it may deepen the ruts in the road leading us back to the very attitudes and behaviors we are trying to escape. If our hope for freedom is based on understanding the reasons why, then many will sink down into despair, feeling powerless, helpless, and hopeless.

Romans 12:2a tells us "Do not conform to the pattern of this world." We often get stuck in patterns of thought which are not in line with God's truth. They are "of this world." In the beginning, we follow these patterns because worldly wisdom convinces us it is the best choice. Over time, the ruts in the path become so deep that our brains go on autopilot. We no longer need to consciously think about it. When our brains process the right combination of inputs, we are quickly whisked along the path back to the destructive behaviors.

When we retrace the patterns which lead to the destructive behaviors, we learn "how" our brains are processing inputs from our world and from our relationships, and we begin to understand how these inputs carry us down the path to the behaviors that feel inescapable.

For most of us, these patterns in our brains become so automatic, we are unaware they exist. We experience the strong pull towards these ongoing behaviors, but over time, we lose track of the steps which make up the pattern repeatedly drawing us back in. Ironically, understanding "why" we return to destructive behaviors and patterns does not help us understand "how" our brains process information and repeat these patterns. The reasons why may explain when the pattern started. They may uncover some of the steps to healing, but the reasons can never fully uncover the patterns which explain how our brains are guiding our choices.

Of course, these patterns in our minds do not force us to behave in a particular way. We still have our God-given ability to make choices. We still have free will. When we are carefully guarding our thoughts, we can choose to steer away from the well-worn paths toward healthier behaviors. Until we find a way to change these patterns, the autopilot responses will remain. Any time we are worn down, discouraged, or simply inattentive, we are at risk of being drawn back into the old patterns and behaviors.

There is hope for us, though! God created us with a way to change these patterns. Science has proven we can structurally re-wire the neuron paths through our brains. This neurological process is called "neuroplasticity." Merriam-Webster defines neuroplasticity as, "The capacity of neurons and neural networks in the brain to change their connections and behavior in response to new information."[2] Stanford University published an article describing neuroplasticity as a phenomenon which "allows the neurons in the brain to . . . adjust their activity in response to new situations or changes in their environment."[3] When we repeat mental patterns in our brain, neuroplasticity allows the patterns to become hard-wired. But are these patterns set in stone? No, they are not!

Neuroplasticity allows our Creator designed our brains. In most areas of our life, hard-wired thought patterns are actually quite helpful. In order for us to function in a world of countless choices, most decisions must be pre-programmed into our brains. For example, when we tie our shoes, the pattern is automatic. We don't think about each loop and knot. When we are driving and see the brake lights on the car in front of us, we automatically move our foot to the brake pedal. We are not consciously aware we are doing this. It is a pattern in our brains keeping us safe from accidents. If we had to consciously recognize the brake light and think through how we should respond, we would not be able to stop in time. Any parent who has taught their teenager how to drive knows how scary this can be. While the teen is learning this new neural network pattern,

---

2   Merriam-Webster, "Neuroplasticity," https://www.merriam-webster.com/dictionary/neuroplasticity. (http://www.merriam-webster.com/dictionary/neuroplasticity)

3   Liou, Stephanie, "Neuroplasticity." *Hopes Huntington's Outreach Project for Education, at Stanford*, https://hopes.stanford.edu/neuroplasticity/. (http://web.stanford.edu/group/hopes/cgi-bin/hopes_test/neuroplasticity)

sitting in the passenger seat without a brake pedal can be an intense experience!

Our brains have developed many thinking patterns which are helpful and healthy. Some thoughts bring fear, making us cautious. Others bring hope, encouraging us to continue to move forward. Thoughts which bring peace remove feelings of worry and allow us to feel at ease and secure. These are all healthy and helpful patterns which occur in our brains. It is the way God made us.

But when we learn and practice patterns that are of the world, we hard-wire those patterns in our brains, creating a well-worn path to the inappropriate and sometimes destructive behavior. These patterns we practice are carried out as quickly and efficiently as the healthy patterns. Whether the patterns are healthy or unhealthy, our brains are working exactly as they are designed. The patterns are carried out exactly as we have trained our brains to operate.

A NEW HOW: CHANGING THE PATTERNS

When we understand how the hard-wired path leads us to inappropriate behaviors, it gives us the opportunity to change and create new pathways through our brains. We become aware of the lies that have infiltrated our core beliefs. We become aware of how our brains take us to the place where the unhealthy behaviors seem reasonable and helpful. As we address and change these core beliefs, we can create new patterns...patterns that are not "of this world." We replace the old patterns with godly and healthy patterns that are based on truth and result in better choices. Creating these new patterns of thinking brings positive emotional and spiritual change in a way that is consistent with how God has designed our brains. It gives us the ability to renew our minds and bring about permanent life change.

Creating the new patterns does not guarantee we will never again make bad choices. We can still choose to go back to the old, worldly patterns, but it is no longer a choice that happens on autopilot.

Peter warns us about these dangers in I Peter 5:8 when he says, "Be alert and of sober mind. Your enemy the devil prowls around like a roaring lion looking for someone to devour."

It is always important to stay alert and aware because our enemy wants to draw us back into worldly patterns. He wants to convince us that practicing these unhealthy patterns is the best way forward. If we believe the lie and choose to practice the old way, it is possible for us to become ensnared once again in patterns which take us down the path to unhealthy or destructive behaviors.

Since God gives us the ability and the responsibility to renew our minds, learning new, healthy patterns is "how" we can renew our minds and bring life change. Once learned, we must be careful to practice and protect these patterns that lead us to healthy choices and behaviors.

GOD BRINGS THE HEALING

> [5] Trust in the Lord with all your heart and lean not on your own understanding; [6] in all your ways submit to him, and he will make your paths straight (Proverbs 3:5-6).

Over the years I have seen many people healed through counseling ministries. But here is the reality: Only God can bring healing. I am not smart enough to know what is truly needed in every situation. I am not wise enough to know how to heal anyone's emotional wounds. I cannot change anyone's heart. If it were up to me and my abilities, few people, if any, would ever find true freedom.

God can bring healing in any way he decides. Some people will spend time by themselves in God's word and find true healing and freedom. For others, medications prescribed by a psychiatrist can be an important part of the healing process. I know someone who struggled in an area of sin for years. One day God said in an audible voice, "You are healed, it is my gift to you." This individual was set free! Praise God! This kind of healing is uncommon, but God knows exactly what is needed for each of us. Only he has the wisdom to know our hearts and what will bring freedom. If we want to find the patterns which will help us renew our minds, it starts with the wisdom found in Proverbs 3:5-6. If we trust in the Lord, He will show us the best path forward!

> when we understand how a thinking pattern leads us to inappropriate behaviors, this gives us the opportunity to renew our minds

HOW THE BRAIN DOES FORGIVENESS

When Matt came to me, he was stuck. He knew many of the reasons why he was repeating the anger and critical spirit demonstrated by his father, but he had no idea how to change. Matt focused so much energy on changing these traits but didn't realize he was only treating the symptoms. He was unaware that bitterness and resentment toward his dad were the root causes. This unforgiveness was eating away at his health, ruining his relationships, and keeping him from experiencing intimacy with God.

I met with Matt for several weeks, and together, we worked through a process of discovery and forgiveness. With God's love and direction, he found freedom from the hurt his father had inflicted. It was amazing how this brought about transformational changes in so many other areas of Matt's life.

Jesus teaches throughout the Gospels that we are to be men and women who forgive those who defraud, hurt, and betray us. As we unpack God's truth, we will find these commandments are more than a directive to "do the right thing." God wants us to forgive because forgiveness brings us freedom. Forgiveness gives us the opportunity to experience God's peace and joy and life to the fullest.

I have seen this play out literally hundreds of times as I've counseled men and women through a forgiveness process. It is miraculous to watch. Psychologists have compiled a huge body of research substantiating the correlation between unforgiveness and a wide range of emotional health issues. It should be no surprise to us that the science of psychology has objectively verified the underlying truth of Jesus' message about the power of simple forgiveness. Nothing else can produce the healing and life change that God gives when we "forgive [our] brother or sister from [our] heart" (Matthew 18:35).

This How Not Why principle is so helpful when it is applied to forgiveness. It is important to unpack the reasons why God wants us to forgive, while also learning how to practice forgiveness. We will first examine how our brain does unforgiveness and deceives us into becoming stuck in this pattern. Then we will learn to practice a process of forgiveness which has helped many find new freedom.

2

the "do-nothing" deception

REMEMBER MATT from Chapter 1 who was deeply wounded by his father? For many years, he carried hurts and emotional scars which molded his character and impacted the way he treated others. He was alarmed when he began to realize how his anger and critical spirit were directed at his girlfriend, but he did not know how to change. This caused a lot of conflict in their relationship, and Matt knew his actions were impacting her in a negative way.

We can understand *why* Matt's wounds fueled his behavior, and we can step back and see *why* this pain impacted the way he treated his girlfriend, but these wounds do not excuse his behavior. In fact, one might say Matt should have known better because he experienced the pain and hurt of his father's mistreatment. He did know it was wrong to treat his girlfriend in the same way, and his awareness increased his responsibility to end the cycle of hurt. Though Matt had a strong desire to change, he didn't know *how* to make these changes.

All of us have been mistreated, deceived, and betrayed to one degree or another. We live in a world of sinners. Every one of us is a sinner. Every one of us is guilty of hurting people. Some, we have hurt *on purpose*. It is not only our enemies we have damaged. For many of us, the people we love the most are the people we have wounded the most deeply. The fact that we have been hurt does not give us an excuse to mistreat others.

> though we will all be victims of mistreatment, the choices we make will determine how the hurt affects us

We should not be too surprised when people mistreat us because we all experience the same reality: there is no way to make it through this life without being hurt and without hurting others. Welcome to the human race.

Though we will be victims of mistreatment in our lifetime, God has given us choices in these situations. The choices we make will ultimately determine how the hurt affects us in the long run. When others deceive, hurt, or betray us, what choices do we have? How do we get past the pain? Is it possible to live free of the hurt and fully enjoy life again? What if they aren't sorry for what they've done to me? Is it possible to build healthy and trusting relationships again?

We probably know at a surface level that forgiveness is the answer. But for many of us, this seems too unfair. Doesn't the Bible teach "an eye for an eye?" (Exodus 21:24) Are we supposed to completely let the person off the hook when they have truly hurt us? It seems unfair. The Bible teaches that we ought to forgive, but it feels like we are being asked to simply pretend like they did not hurt us.

In our minds we may say, *Of course I forgive them*, but if we are able to connect with our true feelings, we realize the pain and hurt are not going away. We still feel deeply offended or even angry at the person. We want to be good Christians—and Jesus said, "Turn the other cheek" (Matthew 5:39). So, we decide we will not seek revenge. We decide to do nothing—we just stay neutral.

But is the choice to "do nothing" and "just move on" truly forgiveness? Is this a neutral decision? Time heals, right? I know it is wrong to seek revenge. Isn't "moving on" a more godly choice?

These are valid questions to process, but this approach does not bring freedom. It is the do-nothing deception at work. Perhaps you make an excuse for the other person…find a plausible reason why they offended you: We all have our own issues, right? Isn't this basically the same as forgiveness? I know I shouldn't take revenge, but won't I get over the hurt in due time?

A friend of mine named Jim, said to me, "I didn't do anything with all this hurt *because* I wanted God to handle it." Jim believed doing nothing was a godly response rooted in his faith. He believed he was forgiving and letting God handle the messiness of the issue. He hoped God would teach this person a lesson, but it seemed like God never acted on his behalf. Jim continued to hurt, and he felt like God expected him to go on carrying the pain and resentment. Like Jim, many find that the do-nothing approach to forgiveness leaves them feeling like they are expected to carry the heavy burdens of past hurts on their own. Over time, they may begin to doubt whether God intends to help them at all.

CASSIE

"Nothing in my life is working. I have dated several guys since my divorce ten years ago, but every relationship ends in a train wreck. I feel like my adult children are always judging me. They don't like my current boyfriend and refuse to spend time with me when he is around. My career has completely stalled. I wonder if my boss is going to keep me around much longer. If I am honest with myself, I am not sure I have anything to offer anyone anymore."

Cassie first went to a trusted spiritual leader at her church. He recommended more time in prayer and suggested she join a Bible study. Cassie participated faithfully because she wanted God's help. She enjoyed the studies and learned a lot from her time in the Word, but little changed. Instead of bringing her relief and a joy for life, she sank deeper. It felt to her like God was ignoring her. She felt even more alone.

As Cassie and I talked in her first counseling session, I began to understand her emotional state. She felt like she was broken and failing in every area of her life. She assumed this was God's punishment for getting divorced—because "Christians should not get divorced."

Cassie wanted healing but had no idea how to find it. She had invested so much time and effort seeking God's help, but no help seemed to arrive. Of course, she knew that God cares about people, but she began to believe, "He must not care about me."

In the sessions that followed, Cassie began to unpack her life. God allowed her to recall memories of the pain she experienced in her marriage. Her ex-husband's unfaithfulness wounded her deeply. He was an alcoholic, who, especially when he was drinking, berated her and mistreated the children. He even blamed Cassie for his unfaithfulness. She internalized many of the awful things her husband said to her and began to believe them. She blamed herself for the way her husband mistreated the children. "Why didn't I do a better job of protecting my kids?" For a long time, she believed that she was a terrible wife and a worse mother.

I asked Cassie, "Have you ever forgiven your husband?"

The question surprised her, "Why? He never asked me for forgiveness. He thinks everything is my fault!"

She didn't feel like she was holding a lot of anger towards her ex-husband and decided moving forward was the best choice. She didn't feel like she wanted revenge. She simply decided to move on with her life. This is exactly what she tried to do for the past ten years.

Cassie was surprised as God began to reveal things about her own heart. She uncovered a lot of bitterness towards her ex-husband. While she did not feel a great deal of anger, Cassie still held many things against him. She often disparaged and belittled him when talking with her children and friends. She blamed him for many of the difficulties in her life resulting from the alcoholism and the divorce.

THE HIDDEN ROOT OF BITTERNESS

Cassie was stuck in a common trap. While desiring to do the right thing, especially as a follower of Christ, many people decide they need to move on with life. We all know it is wrong to seek revenge or try to get back at the person, so we decide the best thing to do is *nothing at all*. We try to "just forget about it." We move on with our lives with the expectation that "time will heal."

The problem with the do-nothing plan is this: we are not actually doing nothing. It is a choice and a response to our pain. When we are hurt, it feels like life is already rolling downhill. When we decide to do nothing, it is like putting the car in neutral on an unnoticed slope. While our attention is focused on "more important" matters, our descent gradually accelerates. The hurt, over time, grows and grows. Eventually it turns into bitterness. There is no other possible outcome. Though it disguises itself in our lives in many different forms, the underlying bitterness will eventually overtake us.

The greatest deception of the do-nothing trap is we often are unaware bitterness is present. We work hard to avoid the powerful desires to get even. We try not to gossip or say bad things about the person. We avoid overt action like trying to even the score. We try to act in the way we think is right, but bitterness grows beneath the surface.

> Look after each other so that none of you fails to receive the grace of God. Watch out that no poisonous root of bitterness grows up to trouble you, corrupting many (Hebrews 12:15 NLT).

The writer of Hebrews says bitterness is like a poisonous root. The plant which grows from it may appear to be beautiful. It may look like a tree of life. We do not hold onto bitterness knowing it is going to destroy us. We hold onto it because we are sure it is helpful.

In our backyard, we have a half-acre of woods. Several years ago, I noticed a beautiful flowering vine growing up through the trees and thought it looked so pretty. I pointed it out to my wife. She loves gardening, so she wanted to find out the name of this beautiful little flower. She quickly discovered the vine was an invasive species which rapidly grows up into a canopy and strangles trees. I immediately cut it off at the base. As I untangled the vine from our trees, I was shocked as I realized this small stem of a vine was choking the sunlight from half of the canopy of trees on my property. Left untended, this vine would have destroyed our beautiful, wooded area!

My wife went to the Department of Natural Resources website to find more information about this vine. She learned the only way to eradicate it is to clear the soil of its entire root system. Clearly, we needed to do more to get rid of this terrible nemesis. A root of the vine can stay dormant in the soil for years before it starts growing again. We could cut down many branches of these vines, one after the other, but eventually, they grow back. The only way to truly eradicate the vines from our yard is to completely remove the root.

It is the same with the "poisonous root of bitterness." Like the root of the vine, we may not even be aware unforgiveness is present. As it grows and begins to choke out the branches of the tree that is our life, we notice the vines. We try to disentangle and cut them down. As long as the root of bitterness remains hidden beneath the surface, the symptoms of unforgiveness eventually creep back in.

> the greatest deception of the do-nothing trap is we often don't even know bitterness is present

And like the beautiful, flowering, yet invasive vine, many even think withholding forgiveness is helping their lives to blossom. Withholding forgiveness may seem like a reasonable or even wise choice. We fear forgiveness will put us back into a harmful relationship. There are many reasonable-sounding justifications which convince us it's foolish, unjust, or even ungodly to simply forgive.

As we will see in future chapters, the desire to hold onto bitterness is based on a fundamental misunderstanding about the nature of forgiveness. The root of bitterness will poison our lives. Some overtly seek revenge motivated by a sense of self-righteousness, but many repeatedly push down their feelings of resentment. Either way, the outcome is the same. Bitterness, like a poison, slowly destroys us.

PART TWO

THE
UNFORGIVENESS
TRAP

3

the unforgiving servant

ONE DAY JESUS was with his disciples, and they asked him a question about forgiveness. He tells the following story about an unforgiving servant. Most of this story makes a lot of sense to us, but this story includes some perplexing ideas. Perhaps Jesus' disciples asked him some of the same questions I would ask.

> [23] Therefore, the kingdom of heaven is like a king who wanted to settle accounts with his servants. [24] As he began the settlement, a man who owed him ten thousand bags of gold was brought to him. [25] Since he was not able to pay, the master ordered that he and his wife and his children and all that he had be sold to repay the debt.

²⁶ At this the servant fell on his knees before him. "Be patient with me," he begged, "and I will pay back everything." ²⁷ The servant's master took pity on him, canceled the debt and let him go.

²⁸ But when that servant went out, he found one of his fellow servants who owed him a hundred silver coins. He grabbed him and began to choke him. "Pay back what you owe me!" he demanded.

²⁹ His fellow servant fell to his knees and begged him, "Be patient with me, and I will pay it back."

³⁰ But he refused. Instead, he went off and had the man thrown into prison until he could pay the debt. ³¹ When the other servants saw what had happened, they were outraged and went and told their master everything that had happened.

³² Then the master called the servant in. "You wicked servant," he said, "I canceled all that debt of yours because you begged me to. ³³ Shouldn't you have had mercy on your fellow servant just as I had on you?" ³⁴ In anger his master handed him over to the jailers to be tortured, until he should pay back all he owed (Matthew 18:23-34).

As I read the stories of Jesus, I often find myself scratching my head. Don't get me wrong, Jesus' stories are shockingly brilliant. But when I am honest with myself, when I actually step out of the

I-am-a-mature-Christian-so-I-should-understand-this mindset, I admit that Jesus' stories sometimes leave me perplexed. The disciples themselves, who spent nearly every day with Jesus for three years, often seemed to walk away a bit confused. Have you noticed? (Check out Luke 18:34, John 12:16, and Mark 4:10, 13) When I read these verses, I imagine a disciple said something like, "OK, Jesus, now what exactly did you mean by *that* story?"

The story of the unforgiving servant is no exception. We don't know the reason, but the man in Jesus' story owed an absurd amount of money to the king. The interest on his debt kept piling up, and the servant couldn't possibly even make the minimum payments. Now, the king was calling in the entire debt, and it was time to pay up. The servant's whole life and family were being liquidated for cash. There was no filing for bankruptcy; a life of slavery awaited him.

The servant threw himself upon the mercy of the king. At this point, the king did something completely unexpected—perhaps even unreasonable: He forgave the debt! This servant, who squandered a significant portion of the king's financial resources and deserved prison, was completely released from his debt and allowed to remain a free man.

Then, on his way from being forgiven, the servant did something totally baffling. He found a guy who owed him a few bucks and demanded immediate payment. When the guy pleaded for a little more time, the servant grabbed him by the throat, then had him arrested and thrown into jail. The servant believed his actions were justified. A guy owed him money, and he deserved to get the money back!

Somehow this story got back to the king. Understandably, the king was very upset. He forgave a debt larger than one could possibly pay back in twenty lifetimes, and this servant couldn't let a guy off the hook for a few days' wages? The king threw the unforgiving servant in jail to be tortured until every cent was paid back.

PEELING BACK THE ONION

On a lot of levels, the spiritual application of this story is obvious. The king represents God. The servant represents each of us. We are all sinners, right? In fact, each of us has piled up a lifetime of sins. God's justice demands payback for these sins. Ultimately, we have sinned against God, and we are hopelessly in debt to him.

Jesus' sacrifice on the cross makes it possible for this debt to be paid. We could never hope to repay what we owe in twenty lifetimes of good works. Jesus paid for all our debts on the cross. So, when we ask Jesus for forgiveness, we are forgiven. Like the servant, God has forgiven a debt we could never hope to repay on our own!

This message Jesus shares with us makes sense. He wants us to forgive others because God has forgiven us. We ought to forgive others. We understand. It is a good lesson.

But wait, immediately after telling the disciples how this unforgiving servant "was handed over to the jailers to be tortured," Jesus made a pretty intense statement. One which—for a long time—I did not understand. Here is the statement: "This is how my heavenly Father will treat each of you unless you forgive your brother or sister from your heart" (Matthew 18:35).

Whoa! Seriously? What does that mean? Because this guy "was handed over to the jailers to be tortured!" The New American Standard Bible translation sounds even worse. It says the servant was "handed over to *the torturers* until he should repay all that was owed him."

Beatings and torture were not an unusual part of the first century prison experience. The New Testament records how jailers often beat and tortured people who were arrested. (Matthew 27:26, Acts 5:40, Acts 16:22-23, and 2 Corinthians 11:25) But why did Jesus choose to include this in this parable on forgiveness? What is the spiritual significance? I don't know about you, but if I take this statement at face value—it raises all kinds of concerns. What do the "jailers who torture" represent? It makes me wonder...doesn't this "torture" sound a bit like hell? Is this guy sent to hell because of his unforgiveness?

The servant clearly repented. We see how he stood before the king and asked forgiveness for his debt, right? He asked God for forgiveness, and it seems he experienced God's forgiveness. Did God, after forgiving the servant, then remove his forgiveness? What are the spiritual implications of Jesus statement?

Now, how do I apply this to my own life? God forgave me. If I refuse to forgive someone else, will God then withdraw his forgiveness? Will I be re-sentenced to hell? How is this consistent with the rest of the Bible's teaching about God's character of love and grace and salvation?

These questions may be pushing this parable a bit past what Jesus is teaching, but there are some real puzzles in this story. I have learned that my confusion is based on a lack of understanding. Jesus is not shallow. He is outrageously brilliant—and his understanding runs deep. The truths God is teaching in this passage are not simple, but as we unpack them, we will learn the truth about the consequences of holding on to unforgiveness.

We will be spending the next few chapters looking deeply into this subject of *unforgiveness*. Together, we'll analyze "how" our brains do unforgiveness, and "how" we are deceived into believing unforgiveness is helpful. Along the way, we will find that the puzzles in this story, which at first seem so confusing, begin to form a clear picture. This story is actually teaching principles which are in perfect step with Jesus' message of unconditional love and grace.

4

the fog of bitterness

SEVERAL YEARS AGO, I flew into Atlanta on a business trip. After a good night's sleep, I woke to find an incredibly dense fog had settled down over the city. I printed out directions to the location (before GPS apps) and set out for my morning meeting. I was fully prepared to navigate the unfamiliar streets of Atlanta, but the fog was so thick I could not see landmarks, road signs, or even street names. I forged on but felt like I was driving in the dark with nothing but a dim flashlight. As I attempted to negotiate the roads with diminished visibility, my sense of direction became more and more turned around. I drove a few miles before I gave up and pulled into a service station. I was completely lost.

With bitterness comes a blindness similar to what I was feeling that day—a fog of judgment. Our ability to see clearly and make good life choices becomes impaired. The fog of bitterness dulls our sense of perspective until it becomes more difficult for us to live wisely.

Decisions about life and relationships become so emotionally charged that we lose some of our ability to discern and make good choices.

In his first letter, John teaches the following,

> [9]Whoever says he is in the light and hates his brother is still in darkness. [10]Whoever loves his brother abides in the light, and in him[a] there is no cause for stumbling. [11]But whoever hates his brother is in the darkness and walks in the darkness, and does not know where he is going, because the darkness has blinded his eyes. (1 John 2:9-11, ESV)

It is not possible to hold onto anger and hatred toward another person without an underlying root of bitterness. John, as a leader of the church, likely pastored others stuck in the fog of bitterness. Perhaps he personally experienced this fog at some point in his own life. The metaphor he uses here is quite simple. Bitterness and hatred bring on a darkness in our minds, which makes it more difficult to find our way in life. We stumble around in the darkness. We may think we are walking in the light and making great decisions, but we are actually suffering from blindness. When we do not get rid of bitterness, when we do not forgive, the fog of darkness affects our ability to make wise life choices. The New Living Translation says it so clearly. "Such a person does not know the way to go, having been blinded by the darkness" (1 John 2:11b, NLT).

Wow. How many times have we read this passage and passed over it without realizing how it describes us? I can't tell you how many people who come to me are completely certain they have made the best choices in their lives. They are trying so hard to do the right things, and don't understand why life is giving them "such a raw deal." They are completely unaware that much of their pain has been caused by their own choices. The fog of bitterness makes it impossible for us to see obstacles only a few feet in front of us.

JENNY

Jenny was unaware of the bitterness that consumed her. It crept in and caused her to feel emotionally detached in her relationships. She longed to experience real intimacy. Jenny realized something was holding her back and decided she needed to be more vulnerable in her next relationship. But the fog of bitterness clouded Jenny's thinking, and she was not making wise choices. Desiring intimacy, she became totally open and transparent with an unsafe person.

Jenny's new relationship brought more disappointment and more pain. In the fog of bitterness, she did not understand how to do intimacy in a wise, godly way. Desiring this deeper intimacy, she shared everything in her life without any filters or boundaries. The relationship became dysfunctional and damaging when the "good Christian man" she was dating took advantage of her openness. Jenny felt betrayed.

> bitterness brings on a darkness in our minds which makes it more difficult to find our way in life

As Jenny broke off the relationship, she lost hope. She decided, "Intimacy is not worth all the pain it causes." Lost in the fog of bitterness, she only saw one reasonable choice left—to retreat even further from any type of emotional intimacy. She decided to keep a safe emotional distance in *all* her relationships.

I wish Jenny's story was only about one young woman who came to me for help, but it is a common theme. Does her story remind you of someone you care about? Do you see some of these themes at work in your own story?

It is a painful place to be. Unforgiveness leads to bitterness, which affects our ability to make wise choices in our family relationships, marriages, parenting, financial dealings, and many of our most important life choices. The fog of bitterness will skew our ability to see truth and wisdom in many areas of our lives. It erodes our ability to recognize the lies of Satan and discern godly truth.

The longer we hang onto our unforgiveness, the denser the fog over our minds becomes and the more we believe the lies we would otherwise never believe.

HELEN AND CLARK

Clark had a great job. He was bringing in well over six figures a year. Helen was a stay-at-home mom who cared for their kids full time. Because Clark's job was very demanding, Helen spent most of her days running the household and taxiing the kids to all their activities and events. Since Helen cared about the financial stability and security of the family, she was careful to run the household on a reasonable budget. As a result, Helen and Clark had been able to invest and save a nice nest egg for their future.

Over time, Clark began to resent his wife for spending her days with their son and daughter. He argued the kids didn't "need" her as much as they did when they were younger. It seemed unfair to him that he was the only wage-earner in the family, and he did not think Helen valued all his hard work. Helen worked very hard for the family and made it possible for Clark to focus on his career, but his resentment continued to grow. As bitterness fogged Clark's reasoning, he became convinced Helen did not do much of anything while he was hard at work all day.

Clark decided his wife needed to learn the value of money. He took away Helen's access to bank accounts, imposed a restrictive weekly budget, and handed it to her in cash each Monday. Out of this cash, she was supposed to feed and clothe the family, keep gas in the SUV, and cover any extra expenses such as taking the kids to a movie, buying school supplies, or entertaining guests at their second home. But whenever one of the kids came to him for money, Clark would give them a big smile and a $20 bill.

Since Clark "worked for a living," he was sure it was reasonable for him to spend money. He would often eat out at nice restaurants or go to sporting events with friends. Spending $200 on a round of golf with his buddies seemed totally reasonable to him. He even purchased a brand new, top-of-the-line fishing boat for himself without consulting Helen!

As you can imagine, this couple was on the road to trouble and ended up in my office. It is easy for us to look at this story from the outside and see how utterly unfair and unreasonable Clark was being, but let's look for a minute at how Clark got to the place where he thought his decisions were both reasonable and helpful.

In the beginning, Clark felt left out because he always had to be away from home while his wife got to spend so much time with the kids. Over time, this turned into resentment and bitterness. At this point, the fog of bitterness was pretty light, but because his resentment went unchecked, it still deceived him. He began to believe Helen was being selfish and perhaps even lazy. In truth, she did the work of a full-time, live-in nanny, a housekeeper, and a caterer combined. Hiring staff to cover these tasks would have cost the family tens of thousands of dollars. But in the fog of bitterness, Clark began to believe Helen was not contributing to the success of the family. This belief, though it was false, became his new baseline of "truth."

Over time, Clark's bitterness continued to grow. The fog thickened and his mind was pulled deeper into self-deception. His actions became more and more controlling, and it all created an incredible strain on their marriage.

By the time I saw them, Clark was certain he was justified in his actions. He was convinced he was motivated by a desire to see the family succeed. He believed his decisions were reasonable and helpful. But in the fog of bitterness, Clark made decisions that hurt his wife and damaged the family. Their marriage was spiraling towards collapse. Clark chose to work through his issues which laid a foundation for reconciliation and healing in their marriage. Without forgiveness, this fog would never have lifted from his mind.

> the longer we hang onto unforgiveness, the denser the fog over our minds becomes

The truth we learn from Helen and Clark's story is applicable to all. We've all been in relationships where we allow hurt to turn into resentment and bitterness. The Bible teaches us that bitterness causes our minds to be robbed of our ability to use discernment. The same fog of bitterness which robbed Helen and Clark of their stable life can also diminish our ability to see clearly and make wise choices. Over time, the fog thickens and becomes more difficult to navigate. Poor decisions damage our relationships. We do not realize it is this blindness which guides our choices and causes even more pain. We begin to wonder, "Why do bad things always seem to happen to me?" Our joy and our hope are slowly drained away. Eventually, we feel like just giving up.

But what if God has given us a clear path out of the fog? What if we allow God to lead us? Can we trust him? Can we trust that he knows how to lead us back to freedom? Is reconciliation even possible? Are we willing to trust Jesus by following his example? Is it possible to forgive those who—in our minds—do not deserve our forgiveness?

5

the cost of hidden bitterness

BITTERNESS: THE EMOTIONAL TOLL

When we do not forgive others, we allow bitterness to creep into our hearts. We want to act in a godly way, so we push down feelings of anger. In an attempt to move on, we convince ourselves that we no longer feel angry. Eventually, though, the suppressed anger begins to bleed out. Often, it is not directed at the person who really hurt us, but toward our loved ones.

Bitterness drives many different emotional problems, such as anger, inability to trust others, emotional detachment in relationships, lack of self-worth, depression, and the list goes on.[1] These emotions are so powerful and so noticeable that they often mask the root cause of

---

1   Mayo Clinic Staff, "Forgiveness: Letting go of grudges and bitterness." *Mayo Clinic*, November 2020, https://www.mayoclinic.org/healthy-lifestyle/adult-health/in-depth/forgiveness/art-20047692

bitterness. While our lives seem to be unraveling, bitterness remains hidden beneath the surface—often unrecognized and undetected. We notice the symptoms and recognize them as emotional problems, depression, or personal character issues.

Though we may be unaware of the bitterness, over time, we become more and more painfully aware of our emotional distress. We may begin to think we have some basic character flaws which make us act out in anger or retreat into depression. We may blame the behavior of those around us. If we are willing to admit our own flaws, we may begin to work on these behaviors. For example, we may think, *If I can just get over my anger... If I can get past my depression...If I can figure out how to move on...then I will begin to experience joy in my life again.*

> though our lives seem to be unraveling, bitterness remains hidden beneath the surface

With these efforts, we may have some limited success, but eventually, it will be overshadowed by a new setback. Remember the vine and its root system in my back woods? It's like we chop down one vine, but the root system hidden beneath the surface is still strong. Consequently, two more spring up in another place. Because we are not dealing with the root problem of bitterness, a new emotional or behavioral symptom invariably emerges. Each new symptom is a setback and makes us feel less able to cope. Eventually we lose hope. We begin to think this is the new normal. We are destined to fight a mostly losing battle with the same emotional problems and character flaws for the rest of our lives.

We feel stuck. We lose hope. And when we lose hope, depression takes hold and begins to overwhelm us. The do-nothing trap of unforgiveness deceives us. We believe we are moving forward when we choose it, but bitterness begins to eat away at us, and we pay a huge emotional, toll.

BITTERNESS: THE RELATIONSHIP TOLL

When I first started to encounter children of divorced parents, I noticed a baffling pattern of behavior. When one parent became distant, the child would often lash out at the parent who remained closer to the child. When I talked to these kids, they clearly knew which parent had hurt them the most, and they recognized and appreciated the parent who was still around and caring for them.

Bitterness, when it causes anger or even rage, is rarely aimed at the people who hurt us. Typically, our rage is directed at the people closest to us, because they are the people we feel safest expressing our emotions to. They have proved they are trustworthy. They have demonstrated they will be there for us, even when things get awful. So, we uncork our emotions, and the people who are doing the most to support us receive the brunt of our bitterness-fueled outbursts.

However, not all of us act out our bitterness in bursts of anger. Others simply decide, *I will never allow anyone to hurt me in this way again!* We circle the wagons in order to protect ourselves. We decide we are going to shut out anyone who may be a potential threat. Since the people we love the most have the power to hurt us the most, we put up walls which are detrimental to our own wellbeing. This decision, often made subconsciously, affects our marriage, our kids, our friends, and all our relationships. We end up shutting out the people in our lives who have demonstrated that they care the most.

I have seen this play out in all kinds of relationships, not only children of separated or divorced parents. Adult children will not talk to their parents. Adult siblings constantly compete and cause family conflict. Business partnerships dissolve. These are real outcomes of bitterness which touch real people's lives.

BITTERNESS: THE SPIRITUAL TOLL

As Christians, we know God loves us. We have heard the promises of joy and hope from scripture:

> "And we know that in all things God works for the good of those who love him. . ." (Romans 8:28)

> "[Nothing] will be able to separate us from the love of God. . ." (Romans 8:39).

> "My purpose is to give them a rich and satisfying life" (John 10:10b, NLT).

We know these promises, and we agree with them. But when bitterness enters our lives, our experience with Jesus is so different. Doubt begins to creep in. Our sense of self-worth erodes. We begin to wonder whether these verses apply to me.

Of course, we would never *say* we doubt the truth of these passages. Those who believe in God know that *God loves everyone*. He offers abundant life to all. But emotional pain and unresolvable character flaws seem to demonstrate they are not worthy of God's love, and they begin to make excuses to explain why God has apparently rejected them.

CASSIE

Cassie believed the message in John 3:16. She believed God loves everyone, but she also believed she "deserved the consequences" she was experiencing. Cassie began to believe God was judging her for her life choices. *It's because I got divorced. God is judging me for being disobedient*, she thought.

Cassie felt leaving her husband was the only viable choice. If she had stayed in the marriage, she knew her children would continue to be damaged, and she might not survive. Even her Christian friends told her she needed to leave her husband. But years after the divorce, she came to believe God was disappointed she ended her marriage. *If only I did something different*, she thought, *I could have saved my marriage and my family.* "It seems like God is not helping me. He must be very disappointed in me," Cassie said.

since the people we love have the most power to hurt us, we shut out the people who care for us

When I asked Cassie whether God can forgive a person who divorces, she said, "Of course. God can forgive anything!" Even though she earnestly believed God forgives, Cassie stopped trusting God would forgive her. I often see this in individuals who find themselves spiritually worn down by the burdens of past hurts. When we get caught in the bitterness trap, we begin to believe we are no longer acceptable to God. No matter how hard we try to find healing, or how devoted we are to our faith, we can still feel alone.

For Cassie, this created intense feelings of loneliness. She felt sure God was pushing her away. Her relationship with God became distant and cold. Most of the time, Cassie felt like he had simply left her altogether. Of course, she believed God's promises were still true, but she said, "They must not be true for me. I must have disqualified myself from the 'full and satisfying life' God promises in the Bible."

Though the thought process and experience may be slightly different for each of us, bitterness does limit God from doing all he wants to do in our lives. The Bible makes it clear that God is not free to move us forward emotionally or spiritually while we are caught in the bitterness trap. This is exactly where Cassie was stuck. Jesus taught:

> "For if you forgive other people when they sin against you, your heavenly Father will also forgive you. But if you do not forgive others their sins, your Father will not forgive your sins" (Matthew 6:14-15).

> "And when you [are] praying, if you hold anything against anyone, forgive them, so that your Father in heaven may forgive you your sins" (Mark 11:25).

Jesus says the Father will not forgive us when we do not forgive others. God wants to forgive us, but our choice to hold onto unforgiveness blocks us from accepting his forgiveness. Bitterness is our attempt to hold control over the entire situation. Our choice to hang onto the unforgiveness may be intentional or unconscious, but God will not override our decision. He only forgives what we allow him to forgive. If we choose to hold onto our judgment, God will allow us to keep it. The fog of bitterness infiltrates our minds, and we give the darkness permission to cloud our thinking. When unforgiveness remains, we are unwittingly hanging onto the darkness. We are making choices which push God and his help away. In the darkness, we cannot see that there is a better way forward.

Doesn't it make sense that Cassie was stuck and felt like God wasn't helping her through the emotional pain and spiritual darkness? Like with many of Satan's lies, Cassie was unaware she was holding onto bitterness.

The problem here is not that God is unwilling to forgive us. Jesus' death on the cross is certainly sufficient to pay for the sin of unforgiveness and bitterness. The Scriptures are clear. When we accept the free gift of salvation, *all* of our sins are forgiven. *All* includes the sin of bitterness.

The problem is this: when we don't forgive others, we are holding ourselves responsible to resolve everything. He wants to treat us in a way that is consistent with his forgiveness, but we do not allow him to.

I believe the truth from these passages is clear. Even though God's love for us remains constant and passionate, even though God wants to fulfill all his promises, our bitterness and unforgiveness prevent God from helping us move forward in these areas of our lives. Over time we become more and more frustrated. When we share our hurts and needs with God, we never seem to get answers. We never feel any relief from the pain. We feel like God has left us, and like Cassie, we may eventually feel spiritually empty, alone, and abandoned.

BITTERNESS: THE PHYSICAL TOLL

Countless studies and research projects have identified a connection between an individual's physical health and unforgiveness or bitterness. "Google Scholar" is a search engine dedicated to scholarly literature. As I was conducting research for this book, I searched this site by entering the phrase "studies linking health and forgiveness."[2] The Google Scholar search engine found over 90,000 links to papers, articles, books, and other scholarly publications!

This area of study, unforgiveness and bitterness, has been thoroughly explored. Scientific and scholarly studies have demonstrated time and time again that there can be some nasty physical consequences for holding onto bitterness. Though experts may have differing interpretations of exactly how or why unforgiveness impacts our physical well-being, there is widespread agreement on the underlying premise: Holding onto feelings of resentment and bitterness can result in a range of adverse physical symptoms.

> when we get caught in the bitterness trap, we begin to believe we are no longer acceptable to God

In a 2001 study, Dr. Charlotte vanOyen-Witvliet, professor of psychology at Hope College, monitored the physiological responses of seventy-one college students as they pictured themselves either forgiving an offender, or as they dwelled on injustices.[3] "When focused on unforgiving responses, their blood pressure surged, their heart rates increased, brow muscles tensed, and negative feelings escalated," she wrote. "It appears that harboring unforgiveness comes at an emotional and a physiological cost."[4]

---

2   https://scholar.google.com/scholar?q=studies+linking+health +and+forgiveness.

3   Valeo, Tom. "Forgive and Forget," *WebMD*, August 2008, https://www.webmd.com/mental-health/features/forgive-and-forget (http://www.webmd.com/mental-health/features/forgive-forget)

4   Ibid

This same Web MD article documents the benefits of choosing forgiveness: "If you can bring yourself to forgive. . ., you are likely to enjoy lower blood pressure, a stronger immune system, and a drop in the stress hormones circulating in your blood, studies suggest. Back pain, stomach problems, and headaches may disappear. And you'll reduce the anger, bitterness, resentment, depression, and other negative emotions that accompany the failure to forgive."

This is a short list of the many physical symptoms correlated with holding onto resentment and bitterness. Unforgiveness does not only impact us spiritually and emotionally, but over time, it also takes a toll on our physical well-being.

A LONG, SLOW SPIRAL DOWNWARD

The bitterness trap is so deceptive. Its consequences rarely come on us all at once. They manifest themselves slowly and over time. At first, we may be able to convince ourselves we are okay. We have moved on. Nothing appears to change for the worse. We may actually feel some sense of relief for a while. Moving on certainly feels better than wallowing in our hurt and the pain of trying to live under those conditions, but hidden bitterness slowly begins to eat away at our soul, our spirit, and our health. Often, it is months or even years before we begin to notice the effects. By the time we realize we need to make changes, the unforgiven offense may be so far in the past that we no longer connect our pain to the bitterness which has taken root.

Bitterness is the root cause for many who come into my office looking for help with their emotional and relationship problems. Most have been carrying this bitterness for years—even decades—and the years of unforgiveness have taken their toll.

6

vengeance: bitterness fully embraced

THERE IS A GROUP of people who whole-heartedly embrace bitterness. Of course, they would never call it by this name. These are the people who believe it is their duty to make things right. It would not be fair to let the offender off the hook when someone has been wrongly treated, and they believe their only legitimate option is to take it upon themselves to make things right.

Satan is a master deceiver (John 8:44). He convinces us that vengeance is justice. As a result, some believe it is our right and duty to even the score, to make sure the person who wronged us understands how much they hurt us. This way, they will know how much it hurts. Then they will learn their lesson and never do it again to us or to anyone else.

I can't tell you how often I hear family members say to one another, "I need you to realize how badly you hurt me."

"Until you understand, there is no way I can forgive you."

"It wouldn't even be right for me to forgive you until you fully understand the extent of my pain."

The real underlying motive in these kinds of statements is clear. If the offender could somehow feel all the pain they made me feel, then I could *possibly* forgive. I must make the offender understand. I will show the offender what this feels like. Only then will moving on be within the realm of possibility.

> when we take upon ourselves God's responsibility to make things right, we are helping Satan to carry out his mission

This is a lie—and it is straight from the enemy. The mindset can be very enticing. How many television shows and movies use revenge as the basic theme for the plot? The hero has been wronged. He cannot rest. . . he will not rest. . .until he finds vengeance. When he finally evens the score and puts the villain down, all is right with the world once again.

All of us have believed this lie at times in our lives, but there are those who decide to actively seek revenge as a lifestyle. Those of us who are stuck in this cycle believe it is our right, even our duty, to pay back the person who has wronged us. Christians can just as easily get caught in this deception. It is the cause of broken marriages, estranged families, and a lot of pain in relationships. In the church, it undermines unity, distracts the body from its God-given mission to make disciples, and fuels church splits.

If this is where you are, then I want you to be aware: You are living a lie. Let me say it again because it is so important. You are living a lie. The enemy of our souls has successfully recruited you to carry out his work and his mission which is the destruction of your life and the destruction of lives around you.

> [26] "In your anger do not sin" [a]: Do not let the sun go
> down while you are still angry, [27] and do not give the
> devil a foothold. (Ephesians 4:26-27)

Is it okay to get angry? Is it possible to do anger without sinning? Of course! There is nothing wrong with anger. In fact, it is a healthy emotion designed by God to make us aware when we see things that are wrong and hurtful. This awareness then gives us the option to respond in godly ways. But it is not godly when we stay in the emotion of anger. When anger remains our only response to hurt, it will turn into bitterness. Anger-fueled bitterness always leads to thoughts of revenge.

Paul wrote this because he knew that when we choose to stay in bitterness and revenge, we give the devil a foothold in our lives. We unwittingly become pawns of Satan. We lash out at the people who have harmed us. They may not even be aware they have hurt us, but we believe it is our moral duty to set everything "right." We believe we are doing God's work, but in reality, we are doing the work of the enemy.

This is why Paul offers these simple instructions:

> Do not repay anyone evil for evil. Be careful to do
> what is right in the eyes of everyone. If it is possible,

as far as it depends on you, live at peace with everyone.
Do not take revenge, my dear friends, but leave room
for God's wrath, for it is written: 'It is mine to avenge;
I will repay,' says the Lord (Romans 12:17-19).

Because we don't know how to do vengeance in a godly way, God
has explicitly given Jesus the position of judge. Our Father has reserved
for himself the job to set things right when we have been hurt. And
God promises he will ultimately set all things right.

When we take God's responsibility and choose to make it our
own, or when we make it our job to make sure they know how bad
they hurt us, then we are not only being disobedient to God, but we
are also falling into the deceiver's trap. This is how we become Satan's
pawns, helping to carry out the enemy's mission.

KING SAUL

I realize these are strong words, but we see this played out in the
stories of the Scriptures over and over. 1 Samuel, chapters 9 and 10
tell the story of how God handpicked Saul to be King of Israel. Saul
was God's guy—his specially chosen man. In the beginning, Saul
was a godly leader. His relationship with God resulted in prosperity
for him, his family, and the entire kingdom. But 1 Samuel, chapters
18 – 31 recount the last eight years of Saul's reign and how he was
controlled by his bitterness towards David.

King Saul spent almost a decade hunting down and trying to
kill David, his most loyal and effective military officer. Blinded by the
fog of bitterness, Saul was convinced he was doing the right thing.
Resentment took root and began to ruin his life. He became "overcome
with an evil spirit" and on multiple occasions tried to "pin David to

the wall" with a spear (1 Samuel 18:10-11). He nearly caused a civil war with Jews fighting against Jews (1 Samuel 28:1-2). At the end of Saul's life, his deception was so complete, he decided he could not trust God. He sought the dark advice of a witch who practiced the occult and summoned demonic spirits for wisdom (1 Samuel 28:4-25).

Saul started his reign as a man of God. He set out to be a godly leader of his people, but he allowed bitterness to creep in. This bitterness caused a profound blindness, which affected his ability to make wise decisions. He embraced his bitterness whole-heartedly and actively sought vengeance.

God told Saul that David was, "A man after [God's] own heart" (1 Samuel 13:14). David proved his loyalty to Saul repeatedly (1 Samuel 24:6; 26:10–11), but Saul in his bitterness could only see David as his archenemy. He began to do Satan's work of destruction by trying to kill David. In the end, David became King (2 Samuel 5:8). The consequences of Saul's desire for vengeance were steep: the death of his own sons, nearly all the men in his extended family (2 Samuel 9:3), and Saul himself (1 Samuel 31:2).

JONAH

Jonah was also a godly man who dedicated his life to serving in full-time ministry as a prophet. He had some pretty understandable reasons to hold bitterness toward the people of Nineveh. The armies of Nineveh didn't just conquer cities and nations. Brutality and mass execution were business as usual.[1] And those lucky enough to escape the sword were often carried away as slaves or exiled (1 Chronicles 5:26). The Assyrian armies of Nineveh used brutality to send a message to all

---

1   Healy, Mark, *The Ancient Assyrian*, (London: Osprey, 1991), p. 54.

nations: submit or be destroyed. Jonah and the people of Israel lived under the shadow of constant threat from Nineveh.

So, when God came to Jonah and told him to head to Nineveh and preach, he wasn't only unwilling, he was offended! These people had every intention to destroy his country, his family, and his way of life. There was no way he was going to be God's agent of mercy and grace to Nineveh (Jonah 4:2-3). These evil people deserved whatever consequences they got.

The result? Jonah embraced his bitterness and ran as fast and as far away as he could from forgiveness (Jonah 1:3). He became irrational and even suicidal (Jonah 1:12). The fog of bitterness so completely blinded Jonah, he was happy to see over 120,000 men, women, and children die in order to carry out his version of justice (Jonah 4:11).

Both Saul and Jonah were convinced they were doing the right thing by embracing their bitterness and seeking vengeance. In the fog of bitterness, they became Satan's pawns. They whole-heartedly began to carry out the will of the evil one. The list of biblical characters damaged or destroyed by vengeance goes on and on: Cain (Genesis 4:1-8), Esau (Genesis 27:41), Joseph's brothers (Genesis 37), Joab (2 Samuel 2:21-38), Absalom (2 Samuel 13:20-38), and Haman (Esther 3-7). All were fixated on making things "right," and all faced the consequences of their bitterness.

THE FAST TRACK TO DESTRUCTION

Jesus was talking about Satan when he said, "The thief comes only to steal and kill and destroy" (John 10:10a). The choices we make and the actions we take when we seek revenge are perfectly in line with the purposes of our enemy. When we take responsibility to carry out "justice," we leave a broad trail of pain and destruction. Sometimes we destroy the lives of those we believe are our enemies. But left unchecked, revenge robs and destroys—not only us—but also the people we care about the most.

If you have decided to embrace bitterness and actively pursue vengeance, you probably do not experience much joy. In fact, you probably don't expect to experience much joy until you carry out your mission for justice. People who make it their mission to set things right, live in the belief that these difficulties will just go away once they find their vengeance. Once their enemies are all put in their place, then life will be better. Joy and peace will return.

It is all a lie—a convincing and very destructive lie. The hurts keep coming throughout our lives, don't they? It is impossible to even the score for every mistreatment we see or experience. Even if we do find some form of justice, we are left disappointed because the anger and indignation do not go away. Life never gets better. The joy never returns. Without forgiveness, life quickly becomes meaningless and hopeless.

> even if we find some form of justice, we are left disappointed because the anger and indignation do not go away

But remember the good news. We have a choice. We all have this choice! God has given us a way to step out of this cycle of bitterness and vengeance. Living in this cycle is like scrambling around a dark room and repeatedly slamming head-first into all the sharp edges. Over time, the self-inflicted wounds we receive as we run around trying to set things right can be more damaging than the pain we feel from the original offense. But when we choose forgiveness, the lights come back on. We are able to see and make better choices. God is then able to begin to heal our hearts. Forgiveness brings hope and illuminates the path back to freedom and joy.

PART 3

THE CASE FOR

FORGIVENESS

7

handed over
to the torturers

IN THE LATE '90s, the Star Wars saga was reborn. The new movies were set as a prequel to the epic Star Wars trilogy of the '70s and '80s. In *The Phantom Menace*,[1] we meet the person behind the Darth Vader mask, Anakin Skywalker. He is a sweet little boy with some extraordinary gifts. We see his love for his mother. We watch as he falls in love with the princess, Padmé Amidala. Anakin becomes a Jedi knight because he wants to be an agent of peace and justice.

But in the third installment of Star Wars, *Revenge of the Sith*, Anakin's mission becomes much more passionate and personal. When his mother is brutally murdered, he decides it is his job to make sure this never happens again to anyone he loves. Bitterness grows inside

---

1   Lukas, George, dir. *Star Wars: The Phantom Menace*. Lucasfilm, 1999. Disney+.

him, and his feelings of resentment begin to feel both logical and helpful. As his plans begin to unfold, he explains to his wife—Princess Padmé—his reasons for betraying the Jedi Order: "I won't lose you the way I lost my mother. I am becoming more powerful than any Jedi has ever dreamed of, and I'm doing it for you. To protect you."[2]

In Anakin's bitterness-fueled quest to protect his wife, he destroys everyone and everything important to him. As the movie plays out, we watch as bitterness transforms the good and caring Anakin Skywalker into Darth Vader, the epitome of evil.

THE TORTURERS?

> In anger his master handed him over to the jailers
> to be tortured, until he should pay back all he owed.
> This is how my heavenly Father will treat each of you
> unless you forgive your brother or sister from your
> heart (Matthew 18:34-35).

We come back to this incredibly harsh statement Jesus makes to his disciples following the story of the unforgiving servant. Handed over to the jailers who torture? Until he pays back all he owes? My heavenly father will treat you the same way?

As we unpack the consequences of holding onto bitterness, this word "torture" no longer seems so over-the-top, does it? When we get caught in the bitterness trap, we are caught in a jail of our own making. In this jail, we experience what it means to be a tortured

---

2   Lukas, George, dir. *Star Wars: Revenge of the Sith*. Lucasfilm, 2005. Disney+.

soul. Here are just a few of the consequences we have discussed in this book:

- Anger and rage
- Foolish life choices
- Lack of self-worth
- Physical symptoms (discomfort, pain)
- Illness and disease
- Broken relationships with family, friends
- Fear of intimacy, emotional detachment
- Worry that God is withholding help or healing
- Depression
- Feeling hopeless, helpless, and worthless

If only this were a comprehensive list of the consequences of bitterness. But, as we have seen, the consequences of living in unforgiveness are far reaching. There is almost no part of our life, our health, or our relationships left untouched when we choose to remain in bitterness.

When we consider the consequences of bitterness, Jesus' imagery of jail and torture do not seem so unreasonably harsh. Unforgiveness ensnares us. When we believe forgiveness is unwise and unreasonable, there is no escape. We experience the painful consequences of bitterness as if we are stuck in a jail cell, we've built for ourselves.

Though it is possible that "his master handed him over to the jailers to be tortured" has eternal implications, it seems clear that Jesus' words are intended to describe the immediate consequences of bitterness in our lives. I have seen it play out in people's lives over and over. Bitterness is the jail cell, and the consequences are the torture.

In the closing moments of *Star Wars: Revenge of the Sith*, Anakin Skywalker is utterly defeated. As he lays injured and near death, his bitterness turns to rage. He has lost his wife. His old friend, Obi-Wan Kenobi, refuses to join him. He is infuriated by the mercy his enemies offer to him. His scarred and broken body is encased in an artificial life-support suit. As the black helmet is clasped down over his head, the transformation to Darth Vader is complete.

When we choose unforgiveness, we put on our own black helmet over our scarred and damaged being. We believe that if we wear this mask of bitterness, it will protect us. It will keep us from being hurt again. Perhaps the mask of bitterness even gives us an advantage over those who practice mercy and leave themselves exposed. Pain skews our vision of the world and keeps us trapped. Instead of being life-giving, it slowly drags us down deeper into the darkness.

A CONFERENCE ENCOUNTER

Dr. Brené Brown has done ground-breaking research on human emotions such as shame and vulnerability. The principles she teaches are incredibly helpful, and it should not surprise us that the truths she learned from her research sound like they have been taken straight from the Scriptures. She communicates these to the world in a way this generation can relate to. As I write this, her break-out TED Talk, "The Power of Vulnerability,"[3] has tens of millions of views and climbing. It is translated into over forty languages and has been viewed all around the world.

---

3   Brown, Dr. Brené. "The Power of Vulnerability." TEDxHouston, Houston, Texas, June 2010. 20:02. https://www.ted.com/talks/brene_brown_the_power_of_vulnerability. *(Note: If you haven't seen Dr. Brené Brown's two TED talk videos on shame and vulnerability, I highly recommend you do. They are worth your time!)*

I was thrilled when I saw Dr. Brown on the list of speakers for a national leadership conference I was attending. I teach many of her principles in churches and classes, and I hoped to hear her next, new nugget of truth. I was not prepared for the boulder that landed on me! Dr. Brown shared a truth which forced me to do a lot of personal soul-searching. Read some of Dr. Brown's own words:

> When you feel judgment—when you judge yourself for asking for help—you are always, by default, judging when you offer help.
>
> I want to say it one more time. When you well up inside with self-judgment because you have to ask for help... That means, no matter what you try to convince yourself, you are judging other people when you offer them help. Because you have attached judgment to needing help.
>
> We cannot give help without judging, when we can't ask for help [for ourselves].... We can't give people permission to ask for grace when we don't give ourselves permission to ask for grace. ... We can't give what we don't have.[4]

I sat in a packed auditorium watching Dr. Brown on a huge screen along with 95,000 others at locations all around the world. But as I heard these words, it seemed like the room suddenly got *very* small.

---

4   Brown, Dr. Brené. "Session 6." Global Leadership Summit 2013, Willow Creek Association, South Barrington, IL, August 14, 2013. MP3.

I felt like Dr. Brown and myself were the only ones in the room, and she was speaking directly to me.

I was in the middle of some difficult financial circumstances. For the first time in my life, I was forced to ask for help. I was unable to meet the needs of my own family without receiving help from others. I hated asking for help. It seemed completely fine when people asked me for help, but I started to uncover a core belief that it was a sign of weakness to ask for help for myself. I never thought of this as self-judgment. But as I took careful inventory of my own heart, God made it clear: self-judgment was exactly what I was doing.

Earning a living always came pretty easily for me. For most of my life, I have been blessed with the ability to give gifts to others in need. It has always been fun for me to send an anonymous envelope with money to help a friend who has a financial need. I love being able to give a grocery gift card to a member of the community who is in the middle of some significant hardships.

So, when I heard Dr. Brown say these words, they were like a punch to the gut. I asked myself, "Could this principle be true? If I hate asking for help, am I judging others when I give help?" It seemed completely ridiculous to me! *I don't judge when I give gifts to others, do I?* But God began to show me that it was true.

THE BITTERNESS BOOMERANG

As I processed this idea in my own life, God began to show me in Scripture how this same principle applies more broadly to unforgiveness. Where do unforgiveness and bitterness come from? Don't they stem from judging a person and holding them in judgement? Unforgiveness is a boomerang we aim at another person, but it always comes back around to ourselves. When we hold unforgiveness against another person, we cannot help but feel unforgiven ourselves. We should not be surprised that Dr. Brown's research supports the truth Jesus taught 2,000 years ago as he spoke to the crowds on the mountainside:

> Do not judge, or you too will be judged. For in the
> same way you judge others, you will be judged, and
> with the measure you use, it will be measured to you
> (Matthew 7:1-2).

For many years, I assumed these words were related to our eternal destiny. While it may be true that this verse is about the final judgment, if this is the only context we consider, then I believe we miss something very important Jesus is teaching about our life and relationships here on earth. It is the principle Dr. Brown discovered in her research after completing and painstakingly analyzing over 13,000 interviews.[5] When we judge others, we can't help but be hard on ourselves. When we are unable to show grace to ourselves in an area of life, we will always attach judgment to others when we see the same issues in their lives.

Here is the principle in Jesus' teaching: When we judge others for their sin, then we judge ourselves with the same severity for our own sins. All of us create core beliefs about which behaviors are "acceptable" and which ones are "unacceptable." These beliefs may come from our upbringing, our friends, the Bible, or even our own moral compass. The problem is this: all of us eventually fall into areas of behavior we believe are "unacceptable."

Of course, we need to judge between right and wrong. The Bible makes it clear that we have the responsibility to recognize and avoid sinful behaviors. It never asks us to pretend sinful behaviors are okay

---

5   Ibid

(Romans 12:9, 1 John 4:1). But in Matthew 7:1-2, Jesus is addressing the temptation to hold another person in judgement. When our core beliefs tell us a sin is not forgivable—that this person should be judged—we fall into shame and self-judgment. As harshly as we treat someone else for their behavior, this is how harshly we treat ourselves when we behave in the same ways.

I am convinced this is an important application of Jesus' statements in this passage. "For in the same way you judge others, you will be judged, and with the measure you use, it will be measured to you" (Matthew 7:2). When we cannot forgive ourselves for our own mistakes, we cannot help but judge others when they make these same mistakes. When we cannot forgive others for their offenses against us, we are unable to show grace to ourselves when we fall into the same behaviors.

> **almost no part of our life, health, or relationships is left untouched when we choose to remain in bitterness**

What would you expect to happen if one of your pastors went to the board and confided that he was struggling with pornography and needed help? Here is what I have seen happen in many churches. The pastor immediately loses his job, and therefore his income cut off. The entire church is told about his sin, and he is immediately ostracized. No one will talk to him. In fact, no one will talk to his wife or kids, either. It is almost like an unwritten rule: everyone in the church talks *about* the family, but no one will talk *to* the family. They are typically forced, or at least "encouraged," to find a new church home.

As a result, the wife often feels like she has no choice but to divorce her husband. She may even want to work on the marriage, but the peer pressure from her church community is too great for her to handle. In addition, her husband is out of work and unable to provide for the family. If she stays with her husband, she and her children will have no friends and no support.

Here is the irony. We could walk into almost any church in America and do a survey of its men. We would get the same basic result: more than half of the men struggle with pornography. These are conservative numbers.[6]

So why do we feel justified to treat a pastor in such an unkind and unsupportive way? Why do we think it is okay for God's people to cast away one of their own in this manner when many struggle with the exact same sin? Some of us may not personally struggle with pornography, but can any of us honestly say we have never had any lustful or impure thoughts? The fact is, at some time in our lives, both men and women are guilty of some kind of sexual impurity. As a result, when we judge another so harshly, we unwittingly put ourselves under the same weight of self-judgement.

We certainly do need to call sin what it is: sin. Sin has consequences that can be severe, and it is unkind and unloving to simply ignore the sin we see in people's lives. I am not sure I know "the best" way to handle the situation described above, but I have seen how this approach has destroyed many lives and ministries.

What do church members, ministry leaders, and other pastors learn from this experience? Many men or women caught up in sexual sin think, *I can NEVER be transparent. I'll lose my job and my marriage,*

---

6   "Pornography Survey Statistics," *Proven Men Ministries* (survey conducted by *Barna Group*), 2014, https://www.provenmen.org/pornography-survey-statistics-2014/ (http://www.provenmen.org/2014pornsurvey/christian-porn-stats)

too. My friends will not only reject me, but they will also turn their backs on my spouse and my children. They determine it is better to stay stuck in their sin than to ask for help and see their life and family destroyed.

And the spouse who is silently suffering may come to this same conclusion. *I hate what my spouse is doing, but is going for help worth the backlash my children and I will have to face?*

And it may not only be our pastor we put in this position. It may be that divorced woman, the unwed teenage pregnant girl, the person who had "one too many" drinks, the guy who sneaks out of church to have a cigarette, or the elder who accidentally dropped the f-bomb playing basketball in the church league. How do we feel about these people? Why do we put them in a "less than" group? Why do we label them for their sins?

It is because we are holding them in judgment. Even though we all have our own areas of weakness and sin, we say to ourselves, *I would never do that.* This judgment has a kind of payout for us, too. When we judge others, it makes us feel better about ourselves in the moment. We would never allow ourselves to think or admit we feel morally superior—that would be pride, after all. But the true underlying motive is similar to the prayer of the Pharisee who was "confident of his own righteousness." We feel thankful we are not like those sinners (Luke 18:9-14).

BLESSED ARE THE MERCIFUL

In Jesus' famous Sermon on the Mount, he started teaching a crowd with some short, proverbs Christians have come to call "The Beatitudes." These little one-liners probably seemed confusing, and Jesus doesn't take any time to explain why they are true. He just serves each one on a platter, unapologetically, and states them as truth. But to the

Jewish people in the crowd, the Beatitudes are so counter-cultural and counter-intuitive, it probably seemed like they were being asked to eat pickled pig's feet!

The fifth statement Jesus makes to the crowd is, "Blessed are the merciful, for they will be shown mercy" (Matthew 5:7). Perhaps this is a statement about how God chooses who deserves mercy when we stand before him some day, but I find this principle to be instructive for how we should live in this life. I see it over and over in the lives of people around me. When we learn to treat others with mercy, it impacts how we allow ourselves to experience mercy in our own hearts.

My son is a high-school soccer player and a bit of a perfectionist. His perfectionism drives him to be better, but it also makes him very critical of himself. He used to leave every game very discouraged, only remembering all the things he could have done better. He has some natural leadership ability and teaching skills, but would always complain, "No one ever listens to me." I could see that when my son was "instructing" other players on the field, his perfectionism was driving him to point out everything they were doing wrong. The underclassmen probably found his comments discouraging and decided it was best to ignore his feedback.

Hoping it wasn't too late, I encouraged my son to change tactics. I said, "Every time you see a kid doing something that could be improved, find something they are doing right and encourage them instead. Always be aware of at least one thing they are doing well so you can point it out."

It is a much more "merciful" and less critical way of handling relationships with a team. My son thought it was kind of awkward at first, but he took the advice to heart and began to point out the good things he saw in his teammates. It resulted in a big change in his relationships and leadership effectiveness. His coach told me he became a "de-facto team captain" because of the influence he earned with his teammates.

And the crazy thing is how much it changed the way my son experienced the game himself. He still made his share of mistakes, but he didn't spend so much time on the field beating himself up. He was able to move on more quickly when he did make a mistake. Yes, my son was still aware of the areas he could improve, but the intense frustration was gone. After each game, he talked about the great plays, the perfect passes, and the successes. He became a better player and enjoyed the rest of his soccer season.

This blessed-are-the-merciful principle that Jesus teaches applies to all our relationships. When we attach judgment to behaviors we see in others, we can't help but judge ourselves for our own failures. When we treat others with judgment, we will assume others are judging us in the same way. Those around us may offer mercy, but our own self-judgment overrules them. We expect and hear judgment even when we are shown mercy and forgiveness.

The same thing happens in our relationship with God. When we judge people around us, we cannot experience the true freedom of God's mercy or forgiveness. Eventually we are guilty of the same kinds of behaviors and attitudes we judge others for, and as a result, we expect and perceive judgment from God. We can read all the Bible passages about confession and God's forgiveness. We can confess our sins 1,000 times, and 1,000 times, God will respond with patience and mercy, yet we will still feel like God is judging us.

This is exactly what happens when we practice unforgiveness and bitterness. "Holding someone in judgement" is a pretty good definition of bitterness. We believe they have wronged us, and it would be wrong to just let them off the hook. We believe it would be wrong to show mercy and forgive, but in our judgment toward the person, we also cut ourselves off from God's mercy. It is not because God stops offering mercy. God does not withhold his mercy. Mercy is a part of his character, which he freely gives to his children. But when we hold others in judgment and refuse to forgive, we reject God's mercy. If our core belief is that people who commit these kinds of sins only deserve judgment, then we believe it would be wrong for God to let us off the hook and forgive us as well. Life is doubly hard when we do not forgive others and cannot receive God's mercy!

A WAY OUT OF THE JUDGMENT CYCLONE

Jesus teaches this counter-intuitive principle; when we judge others, we only experience judgment for ourselves. It is like a cyclone which goes around and comes back around to us. It grows stronger and more forceful over time. Self-judgment fuels our judgment of others. Likewise, judging others fuels our self-judgment. This tornado becomes more and more powerful, leaving a broad path of destruction. It eventually wrecks us and our relationships.

> when we cannot forgive others, we will be unable to show grace to ourselves

How have you seen this play out in the lives of people who you love? Or in your own life? How has this altered the trajectory of relationships? How has it impacted those who live in proximity to this cyclone of bitterness? How long will this continue? If you are struggling with this, take heart, there is hope. There is a way to rebuild trust and develop strong, healthy relationships again.

The way out is mercy and forgiveness. The amazing truth is that we can escape this cyclone if we stop adding fuel to either part of this equation. If we learn to forgive ourselves, then offering mercy to others becomes a reasonable option. If we learn to forgive others, we will allow ourselves to accept the mercy offered to us. Through time—as we repeatedly respond with mercy—forgiveness will become almost automatic. As we choose to forgive others, self-judgment begins to lose its power. We put ourselves back into a place where we can experience God's mercy and forgiveness. We are released from the "jail" and from the "torturers." We have a chance to begin to experience what Jesus promised His followers in John 10:10. We put ourselves in a place where we can begin to live the abundant life.

8

is forgiveness just?

"THAT'S NOT FAIR!"

Dave was furious with his wife—and for good reason. Janice traveled a lot for business. Dave began to suspect some of her trips were not business related. He started asking her if she was having an affair. She denied it, but eventually the truth came out. Dave was devastated.

"There is NO WAY I could ever forgive her," Dave told me. "It's just not fair. She is the one who slept around, and I am the one who is dying inside."

Dave was so hurt and angry he wanted to get even. Janice betrayed him, and he wanted justice. He knew it would be wrong, but he even considered having an affair himself—just to even the score. Forgiveness was out of the question. He felt like he was being asked to give Janice a free pass. It seemed completely unreasonable to Dave. "If I have biblical grounds to divorce her, why should I forgive her?" he demanded.

Dave had a strong desire for fairness and justice. He wanted Janice to experience all the pain he felt. Fairness demanded Janice suffer the same way she caused him to suffer. In Dave's mind, this was the only way he knew to move forward. Anything else seemed unfair.

WHAT'S WRONG WITH JUSTICE?

Is it wrong for Dave to want fairness and justice? Does Janice get a free pass? If Dave forgives Janice, isn't he letting her get away with her sin without any consequences? Doesn't he need to protect himself so she cannot hurt him again? Shouldn't he get a divorce? Doesn't Jesus say divorce is right in the case of infidelity? (Matthew 5:32)

> forgiveness is choosing to trust God to bring justice to the offender and giving him responsibility for the offense

In the past couple of decades of working with individuals, one thing has become clear to me. Many Christians do not understand forgiveness or its power to heal. Many who seem to have a strong doctrinal knowledge of forgiveness often get stuck when they attempt to apply this in their own relationships.

I work with both brand-new believers and mature Christians. I work with those who know little about the Bible one day and another day, with seminarians who have doctorates in biblical studies. We all know forgiveness is good and right, even important, but many do not understand *how* to forgive in a way that is biblical and brings healing.

Of course, I also meet many Christians who *do* know how to practice forgiveness. For these believers, the process of forgiveness is not even something they need to think about. If you asked them, "How do you forgive others?" They would likely respond, "What do you mean? I just forgive them!" Many believers do practice biblical forgiveness and experience God's healing and freedom. These same people are completely unaware that other believers do not have the same understanding or experience. These competent forgivers are often unable to explain to others how they practice forgiveness.

For many of us, the confusion around forgiveness is related to these questions of fairness and justice. How could a good and just God expect me to pretend like I wasn't deeply hurt by this person? Wouldn't this be a dysfunctional response? How do we work out the obvious tension between our need for justice and God's directive to forgive?

A JUST GOD

Make no mistake—God is just. He is perfectly just. The Scriptures make this very clear:

> "because he has fixed a day on which he will judge
> the world in righteousness by a man whom he has
> appointed. . ." (Acts 17:31, ESV)

> "And will not God give justice to his elect, who cry
> to him day and night? Will he delay long over them?"
> (Luke 18:7, ESV)

In fact, God is not only just, but his character also does not allow him to carry out any action which is not completely just. 1 John 1:5

says, "God is light; in him there is no darkness at all." God's fairness is perfect, and his justice is righteous. We can count on that!

MADE IN GOD'S IMAGE

As humans, we do have a desire for justice. We don't need to look far into our own culture to see how true this is. Actors like Dwayne "the Rock" Johnson, Arnold Schwarzenegger, Jackie Chan, Jean Claude Van Damme, and Charles Bronson built very successful careers around "vigilante justice" genre of films. Millions of dollars are spent at the box office to watch these movies. Why? Because we all see the injustice and we want it to be made right. No one likes to see the innocent mistreated, and the perpetrator must be stopped from hurting others.

This strong desire for justice was created in us by God. This makes sense because God is a God of justice, and we are created "in his image" (Genesis 1:26-27). He instilled in us a desire to see justice for others and for ourselves. We want to be treated fairly and we want others to be treated fairly. It is a good—even godly—trait, which God himself instilled in us.

We don't always know how to process the strong feelings that come with our innate desire for justice. Bitterness is inevitable when our desire for justice becomes the most important driving factor in our response to offenses against others or ourselves. It is important we do not allow our need for justice to take control of our decision making. Making justice our primary focus can easily lead us into sinful responses and actions.

So, our need for justice and fairness is instilled by God, yet he clearly instructs us: Forgiveness is the only healthy way forward. Janice's adultery hurt Dave deeply. In the midst of his anger, forgiveness seemed unjust and unfair. This tension between justice and forgiveness can seem irreconcilable. How can God expect us to forgive when we have clearly been wronged? After all, God is the one who created us with a desire to be treated fairly!

True forgiveness must meet God's perfect standard of justice. This is an important point which transformed my understanding of forgiveness. There cannot be true forgiveness unless the perfect and holy justice of God is fully satisfied. So, where does this leave us? Any tension between a need for justice and feelings of unfairness is based on a false understanding of godly forgiveness. True forgiveness is not only compatible with justice, but it must leave room for God to bring justice to everyone involved in the situation. When we forgive others, God does not expect us to simply roll over and take another beating. His justice requires that both the offender and the victim are treated fairly. Forgiveness does not mean the offender is off the hook. God's justice requires consequences for hurtful actions.

RECONCILING JUSTICE AND FORGIVENESS

Forgiveness doesn't mean the offender walks free. It simply means it is not our job to carry out the justice. When we forgive, we are giving up control over *when*, *where*, and *how* justice is carried out. We are letting go of our feeling of annoyance and irritation.

We are deciding to give God—who is perfectly just—full responsibility. God is trustworthy. We are choosing to trust Him to carry out the justice.

As we read earlier in Romans 12:19, "Do not take revenge, my dear friends, but leave room for God's wrath, for it is written: 'It is mine to avenge; I will repay,' says the Lord."

Forgiveness is choosing to trust God to bring justice to the offender and giving him responsibility for the offense. The perpetrator may face the full consequence of their sin in this life or in the next. God may bring justice through punishment, or God may bring justice through his forgiveness.

Jesus came to earth and died on the cross as a sacrifice for our sins. His suffering and death placed the debt of justice, which we deserve, upon his shoulders. Though it is incomprehensible to us, as Jesus hung on that cross, he literally felt the weight and the pain of our sins. All of us have experienced betrayal. All of us know what betrayal feels like. It is heavy, and it is painful. When Jesus took our sins upon himself, this included all the weight and pain of the betrayal and sins committed by us throughout our lives.

> ⁴Surely he took up our pain and bore our suffering, yet we considered him punished by God, stricken by him, and afflicted. ⁵But he was pierced for our transgressions, he was crushed for our iniquities; the punishment that brought us peace was on him, and by his wounds we are healed. ⁶We all, like sheep, have gone astray, each of us has turned to our own way; and the Lord has laid on him the iniquity of us all (Isaiah 53:4-6).

The punishment we deserve was directly transferred to Jesus on the cross. God allowed his own son to suffer in order to provide a way for us to have a restored relationship with him. Those of us who choose to submit to Jesus, to confess our sins to him, and to accept his payment for our sins will experience God's forgiveness. This forgiveness is only possible because Jesus carried out justice on our behalf as he suffered on the cross and died. 1 John 1:9 says, "If we confess our sins, he is faithful and just and will forgive us our sins and purify us from all unrighteousness."

God may ultimately forgive the offender who hurt us deeply. But can we trust God to be fair with us? In order for us to have a relationship with God, we must accept his forgiveness for the betrayal and the sins we have committed. So we should not be shocked or upset if the God of love decides to do the same when our perpetrator confesses with a pure heart. Forgiveness is trusting God to be the perfect judge who knows the heart of the offender and what is needed to bring justice. It is neither our responsibility nor do we have the wisdom to ensure what measure of justice is carried out. This is God's responsibility. When we forgive, we can be confident true justice is being carried out by God! Someday, we will be in heaven with God. If he decides to show us how he brought justice, we will be in awe of his wisdom to be sure. We will be completely satisfied that justice has been served.

VENGEANCE VS. CONSEQUENCES

Does forgiveness mean all the offender's consequences go away?

When we forgive, we are bringing our charges to God and giving him responsibility to bring appropriate judgment to the offender. We are trusting God to carry out appropriate judgment on our behalf. He may choose to do this through natural consequences, or he may do this through punishment. The Scriptures tell us, "Do not be deceived: God cannot be mocked. A man reaps what he sows" (Galatians 6:7). Paul is stating in this passage that consequences follow bad behaviors.

A few years ago, I worked as a business consultant. One day, my co-worker, Joe, pulled me aside to ask for some advice. He said,

"I know you are kind of 'religious,' so I have a question for you. Fifteen years ago, my sister was murdered. There is a parole hearing for the murderer in a couple of weeks, and the parole panel asked me to make a statement. I believe the guy deserves to be in jail and is still a danger to society. But if I testify against this man, am I being vengeful? If I have truly forgiven him, is it wrong to testify against him and try to keep him in jail?"

At some point during those fifteen years, Joe chose to give up the vengeance and the bitterness and forgive the murderer. Though it was his desire to leave the consequences to God, he still had a personal responsibility to be a part of the legal process. I explained to Joe that he could forgive the murderer yet still testify against his release in good conscience. Joe chose to allow God to be responsible for the offense and to oversee the outcomes of the legal process. He decided it was appropriate to testify truthfully about the ongoing effects of the murder on his family and allow God and the authorities God put in place to carry out judgment (Romans 13:1).

A more complete understanding of forgiveness and God's justice removed the fog of bitterness for Joe. It gave him clarity and freedom to testify to the parole panel accurately and honestly. It was important for Joe to be a part of the legal process and to help keep this man from harming others. To be clear, Joe was still leaving the responsibility for judgment in God's hands, but he realized his testimony helped the parole board obtain all the facts needed for a ruling which would protect the community.

Giving responsibility to God does not mean we must avoid doing our part to ensure that consequences are carried out. Often, it is our God-given responsibility to engage in a process which will bring appropriate consequences. For example, a good parent will want to forgive their child, but forgiving does not mean the parent should withhold punishment. Any parent who truly loves their child will use both rewards and consequences to help them learn better behavior. In fact, it is extremely helpful for the parent to forgive the child before a punishment is given. This will help safeguard the parent from inappropriate actions caused by anger or bitterness. Forgiveness will remove bitterness and give a parent the freedom to thoughtfully respond with reasonable consequences which will bring positive change and growth in the life of their child.

Often, it is our responsibility to participate in the formal consequences an offender must face, even after we have forgiven the offender. This may include legal proceedings, financial penalties, insurance claims, documenting incidents with human resources, etc. Whether we are in a position of authority or hold the role of a subordinate, we may have some responsibility in the process. We might be the authority figure who needs to decide on or carry out the consequences for the offender. We may need to put boundaries in place to protect ourselves from a boss or a parent who has proven themselves to be unsafe. Forgiveness will give us clarity of mind to make wise decisions as we identify and implement appropriate consequences.

> forgiveness is trusting God to be the perfect judge who knows the heart of the offender and what is needed to bring justice

A SURPRISING WAY FORWARD

Janice's affair forced Dave to make some difficult choices. I never told Dave divorce was not an option. He knew Scripture gave him full permission to divorce his wife because of her infidelity. As I listened to his situation and his pain, I said to Dave, "I don't know whether God wants you to stay with your wife, but I do know this: regardless of how your marriage ends up, you need to start with forgiveness. If you hang onto your bitterness, you will make a lot of poor decisions, and your decisions will hurt you much more than they will hurt your wife."

I reminded Dave, "Forgiving your wife is not letting her get away with her betrayal. Forgiveness is deciding she is accountable to God for her sin. Whether you decide to divorce your wife or try to work out your marriage—you do not want to start making life decisions without first forgiving her. Forgiveness will give you the freedom to listen to advice, make wise choices, and find the best path forward."

Dave did decide to trust God and forgive Janice. As he gave God responsibility for his wife's sin and betrayal, his infuriation started to melt away. Of course, Dave still felt a lot of hurt and pain, but the fog of bitterness which clouded his mind began to clear. He stopped using Janice's infidelity against her to win every argument. Getting even by having his own affair no longer seemed like a wise choice.

In time, God began to reveal some real issues in their marriage. As Dave's heart softened, he saw how these issues in their relationship contributed to Janice's inappropriate choices. He began to understand some of the reasons she started to look outside their marriage to find intimacy and self-worth. Dave took responsibility for the areas he needed to change in his own life.

When I first met with Dave, I didn't know whether the marriage would survive, but it was amazing to see how God intervened to bring about amazing healing. I watched as Dave trusted God enough to allow forgiveness to do its work in his own heart. The marriage became stronger than ever. They are still married today and have a Christ-centered family, serving together in ministry. Dave and Janice now work hard to be attentive to one another's needs. The love and joy they share shines so brightly!

9

false forgiveness

MY FAMILY LOVES Walt Disney World®. What do we love about it? We love *everything* about it! We love the atmosphere. We love the adventure of feeling like we are discovering new and exotic places. We love making memories as a family. For us, it feels like the place where dreams really do come true.

When I had the opportunity to get a job in the Magic Kingdom as a college student, I jumped at the chance. It was amazing to work behind the scenes and witness how all the actors, employees, and products work to create a magical day for all the park guests.

A visitor's first time stepping onto "Main Street USA" and taking in the view with all the shops, attractions, and Cinderella's Castle is truly breathtaking. The decorations, the music, the Disney characters, and the architecture create the sights and sounds that make you feel like you have been transported into a movie.

Only a few steps away, through the "Cast Members Only" door, there is another world unknown to the average guest. The buildings which create the illusion of a total wonderland are ordinary buildings. The unseen tunnels beneath the park lead you to storage rooms, walk-in freezers, water pumps, delivery trucks, recycling receptacles, and of course, security guards. It is "wonderland" to "warehouse" in a matter of steps.

Disney would be the first to admit that when we walk through the gates at Magic Kingdom, we are stepping into a false reality. They created this beautiful façade for people to escape to and enjoy their time together. They spend a lot of time, effort, and money to create this illusion for its millions of guests. When we take the boat through "Pirates of the Caribbean," we don't realize we are floating in a big circle through a huge industrial building. Behind this false front is a team of talented designers, a marvel of modern engineering, and thousands of guests who want to be immersed in the experience.

False forgiveness has many parallels. It has all the appearance and dressings of forgiveness. It may even be based on a good sermon or well-meaning advice from Christian friends. We put a lot of effort into it. We are earnest as we practice it. But in the end, we still feel stuck. When we practice a false form of forgiveness, we still carry the burden of responsibility. The pain and bitterness do not go away.

FORGIVENESS MYTH #1: FORGIVE AND FORGET

I was being interviewed by Bill, a Christian organization's board member. He asked me some basic questions about my faith and relationship with God. As we discussed different topics, Bill wanted to be sure we agreed on some foundational biblical principles. "I want to make sure you are in line with our doctrine on forgiveness. I am sure we both agree on the importance of the biblical mandate to 'forgive and forget.'"

For most people in our culture, the default definition of forgiveness is: "Forgive and Forget." It's age-old advice, and a memorable bullet point in a sermon. It's easy to understand and apply. It sounds reasonable and helpful—even spiritual.

Of course, we know we cannot actually forget the offense. We try to apply this principle by treating the offender as if they never hurt us. Isn't this biblical? Isn't this what Jesus taught when he said we should "turn the other cheek" in Luke 6:29? Hebrews 8:12 says God "will remember their sins no more."

Coming from my background and experience in counseling, I have seen many people hurt by this kind of advice. I could not let this discussion with Bill go without addressing it, so I responded, "First of all, I pray this never happens to you, but let's say one of your parents sexually molested your child."

Bill quickly replied, "That would be awful!"

I agreed, "Yes, so awful it's hard to imagine, but at some point, you would need to come to terms with the offense and forgive them, right?"

Bill thought about this for a minute and responded, "Yes, I believe God would want me to forgive them."

"But would you ever leave your kids alone with your parents again?" I asked.

Bill's answer was immediate, "Absolutely not!"

"Right," I said. "But isn't this the way we expect others to practice forgiveness. Just forgive and forget about it. If you truly "forgive and forget" your parent's abuse, wouldn't you treat them like nothing had ever happened, like they never molested your child? Before that happened, you probably would have trusted your parents to care for your kids, right?"

"Well, that's an extreme example!" Bill said defensively.

"Agreed," I responded, "but it is a real-life example from my counseling office. And I have encountered many other individuals abused by spouses, mistreated by friends, or betrayed by someone they trusted. Should they 'forgive and forget' the betrayal and put themselves in harm's way again? I hope no caring person would recommend something so unsafe and foolish."

Bill's thinking was challenged that day, and I give him credit for being open-minded enough to reconsider his stance. Unfortunately, though, well-meaning Christians give this kind of advice to vulnerable and hurting people all the time. When we pretend no offense has taken place, we run the real risk of putting ourselves directly back in harm's way.

Unfortunately, people who try to forgive and forget often end up in my office. It can be very detrimental when these hurting individuals try to treat the offender as if they never hurt them. People who hurt us once will likely hurt us again. Forgiveness is choosing to trust God to bring justice to the offender. It is *not* forgetting. It is *not* treating the offender as if they never committed the offense. When we are hurt, it is important and even godly to put healthy boundaries in place in order to protect the people we care about—as well as ourselves—from the perpetrator. Trust must be earned. It is foolish for us to blindly trust someone who hurt us.

Does God expect us to forgive when someone hurts us deeply? Certainly, but even God does not ask us to forgive and forget. David faithfully served King Saul as a soldier. His military service started with the slaying of the giant named Goliath, and he continued to prove his loyalty as a great warrior and protector, commanding the armies of Saul. When Saul repeatedly tried to kill David, he fled from Saul (1 Samuel 20-21). In fact, David spent about eight years running from Saul. During this time, he heard from God many times (1 Samuel 23:2-3, 4, 9-12; 30:8), but we never read that God asked him to return to serve in the house of King Saul.

Did David forgive Saul? We see from David's actions—he did choose to forgive Saul by giving God responsibility for the injustice. On two separate occasions Saul was completely helpless, and David could have killed him, but David made it clear he trusted God to bring Saul to justice (1 Samuel 24, 26). While standing over the sleeping king, David said to his loyal soldier, Abishai, "You must not harm him! ... I know that the Lord himself will kill Saul, either when his time comes to die a natural death or when he dies in battle" (1 Samuel 26:9).

David could have taken his revenge. He was no stranger to killing those who preyed upon the innocent or the enemies of God. The song "David has killed his tens of thousands" (1 Samuel 8:17) may have been an exaggeration, but he definitely earned the reputation. Even though David could have easily killed Saul himself, he trusted God to wait for him to bring Saul to justice. It seemed unimportant to David *how* God brought Saul to justice, but David trusted God to be the perfect judge who knew Saul's heart and knew what was needed to bring justice.

God expected David to *forgive* Saul, but that didn't mean he expected David to *trust* Saul. God did not expect David to forget that Saul was trying to kill him. Even when Saul swore he would never harm or hunt David again, he did not return to live with Saul. David retreated back into hiding (1 Samuel 24:22; 26:25). David did not act as if no offense was ever committed. He knew Saul was not trustworthy. Though he certainly hoped Saul would abide by his promises to stop trying to kill him, David stayed away at a safe distance to watch and see if Saul proved to be trustworthy.

Trust *can* be restored. Our friends and family will do and say things that offend us. Hurtful things are often said in moments of weakness and anger. These minor offenses happen to all of us, and the reality is we are all guilty at times of saying hurtful and offensive things. In these cases, it is reasonable to forgive and continue the relationship.

But when we face the really deep hurts that come from betrayal, being repeatedly offended, belittled, or physically threatened, protecting others and ourselves from further or additional harm is critical. Along with forgiveness, we may also need to put healthy boundaries in place in order to protect us from being hurt repeatedly.

FORGIVENESS MYTH #2: MAKING EXCUSES

"I understand why my dad yelled at me all the time. Compared to the way Grandpa and Grandma treated him, he was a great parent!"

"Sure, my boss berates me, but it is easy for me to forgive him because he is under so much pressure!"

"Of course, I forgive my son for getting a DUI. Young kids do stupid things..."

"I can forgive my wife for running up our credit card bills. She usually is buying things she feels the family needs."

We live in a culture that loves to give second chances. This, in many ways, is a good thing. We hope to see people redeem themselves and improve their lives. We know that many people are helped when an individual changes the course of his or her own life for the better. For example, when a drug addict gets clean and sober, this will improve the quality of his or her life. In addition, their family will be able to find stability and have hope for the future. Even the community benefits when a citizen becomes a healthy contributor to society instead of a drain on public services and law enforcement resources.

We often ask, "Why?" Why does this person treat me this way? What is their family background? What is their socio-economic situation? How have personal relationships impacted their decision making?

For example, whenever there is a terrible crime committed—such as a murder—one of the first questions everyone wants to understand is, "Why?" Why did the killer commit such a terrible crime? What thoughts made committing such a horrific act seem reasonable to the killer? How could we as a community have identified these behavioral anomalies and prevented this tragedy?

Even our court systems alter the punishment of criminals based on "mitigating factors." A woman who kills her abusive husband is likely to receive a lesser sentence from the judge than the criminal who murders a complete stranger in cold blood. Why? Because as a society, we believe that when a person is hurt and victimized, these experiences can damage the person emotionally. This psychological damage explains the motives behind otherwise appalling behaviors. Survivors of traumatic victimization may actually feel like they must mistreat others in order to even survive. Though this kind of abuse does not justify the crime, we believe these "mitigating factors" can strongly influence a person towards behaviors which may harm others.

There is some truth to this line of thinking. When a person is victimized, it probably will impact their emotional health and decision making in some way. The court system may or may not be justified in the way it hands out sentences. People's family, upbringing, or socio-economic situation can have a significant impact on a person's choices and behaviors. The purpose of this discussion is not to debate the extent to which these ideas may or may not be true.

To be sure, taking the effort to understand the other person's point of view can be helpful. This can give us a more accurate and reasonable perspective of the situation. The problem for many of us, though, is this thought process defines the way we practice forgiveness. Often, we try to justify the actions of the person who hurt us. We try to identify the reasons that caused them to mistreat us. We even question how we may be partially responsible for provoking the unreasonable and hurtful behavior. When we have found strong enough reasons to justify the hurtful behavior, we feel like we have forgiven the person.

This kind of false forgiveness is often part of a cycle of abuse. The excuses create an environment that minimizes the harmful behavior and makes the victim feel responsible for the abuse. The abuser is enabled to continue the abusive behavior. We often see this played out, not only in abusive relationships but also in the lives of children and spouses of alcoholics. When a victim of abuse is willing to accept these kinds of excuses as valid, the cycle of abuse continues unchecked. The outside help—which is needed as a lifeline for change and healing—is not sought out or taken seriously.

Making excuses for hurtful behavior is not the kind of forgiveness that will bring freedom. When we make excuses, we do not practice the forgiveness taught in the Bible. Though our heart may be in the right place, we end up holding on to the offenses we have minimized or excused. False forgiveness deceives us, and the bitterness, anger, or resentment stays with us. We remain stuck.

SETH AND REBECCA

Seth and Rebecca were married for ten years. Seth came into my office feeling extremely frustrated with Rebecca. She had a serious drinking problem. Even though Rebecca had sought help and taken steps to bring an end to her addiction, to Seth, the pain was still present. He thought he forgave her, but his irritation seemed to keep growing. Seth said, "Sometimes Rebecca came home on a Friday night after having a few glasses of wine. Actually. . .she often had a few too many, and the next day, she was hungover, grumpy, and self-centered. She told the kids and me to stay away most of the day—until she felt better."

> if forgiveness is trusting God to bring the person to justice, then making excuses for the person is not forgiveness at all

Seth continued, "Rebecca's doing a lot better with her drinking. I know her mom was an alcoholic, and her job is so stressful, so she can't help her addiction. Of course, I forgive her, but I still find myself avoiding her. I seem to have a very short fuse when I am around her. I can't get past the way she treated the kids and me!"

If forgiveness is trusting God to bring the person to justice, then making excuses is not forgiveness at all. These excuses are only an attempt to negotiate a kind of justice that simply lets the person off the hook for hurtful behavior.

Seth had some very convincing reasons why his wife drank too much: a stressful job, an alcoholic mother, etc. As the two of us talked, he began to realize all these "reasons" were simply rationalizations for her poor behavior. In his attempt to forgive his wife, he was simply trying to convince himself her past behavior was not so bad and perhaps not even her fault. Since Rebecca had little or no choice, he felt like he should forgive and move on.

Making excuses sidesteps forgiveness. It is an attempt to make forgiveness unnecessary. When we try to explain away the hurtful behavior with excuses, we are trying to trick our minds into believing the offender is not guilty at all. If the offender is not guilty, then there is nothing to forgive! We believe forgiveness has occurred. In reality, we stuff the offense into a backpack, strap it onto our backs, and unwittingly carry this heavy, painful load around with us.

It's crucial to accept that we have been wronged. If we cannot accept this, then the forgiveness transaction between God and me does not occur. If we cannot admit to ourselves that the offender actually committed an offense, then why would we need to forgive them? We can only forgive if we believe a wrong has been committed. Making excuses for the offender is like sweeping the offense under a proverbial rug. It may even feel better to us for a time, but eventually it will come back and trip us up.

Our motive for accepting the offender's guilt is not to seek revenge, nor is it because we believe we know how to set things right. Our motive is forgiveness, allowing God to bring his justice to the person and the situation. When we recognize that a real offense has taken place, only then are we able to release it to God's control.

As Seth began to see how he was making false excuses for Rebecca's drinking problems, it became obvious her past behavior still caused him a lot of pain. He began to recognize that he needed to admit how her past behavior was hurtful to her family. Only then was Seth truly able to forgive Rebecca. His choice to forgive his wife dramatically changed their relationship, primarily because it allowed him to see his wife differently. Forgiveness removed the fog of bitterness that clouded Seth's eyes. His anger changed into thankfulness, and Seth was able to tell her how much he appreciated the way she took control over her drinking. It was fun to see how God used true forgiveness to transform a struggling relationship into a caring family full of joy.

FORGIVENESS MYTH #3: TIME HEALS

People often say it to wounded friends: "Time heals." It is a great one-liner, and, of course, it is well intentioned. We believe it to be a common-sense truth. After all, it is true in our physical bodies. God has designed our DNA with the amazing ability to self-heal. When we contract a sickness or receive a physical injury such as a broken bone, time is required to complete the healing. Our bodies have been designed to participate in the healing process and bring us back to health. A cut or a broken bone, with some modest care, will heal over time. Our bodies know how to fight the common cold. In fact, they seek out and destroy these virus cells so proficiently, most doctors will not prescribe any drugs to fight these sicknesses. "Wait a few days—possibly a week—and let the cold run its course," they say. Time is the best treatment for many physical ailments and injuries, but when emotional wounds turn to bitterness, it is more like a cancer than a virus. When cancer is left untreated, time is no longer the hero. If we allow it to grow, it will take over our entire physical bodies. When time is applied as the treatment for cancer, the end outcome is almost always death.

"Time heals" is advice friends and advisors offer because they want to be hopeful. It sounds like sage advice when we don't know what else to say. In other words, just be patient and things will get better. This common advice tells us, "Eventually the pain will lessen. Eventually the hurt will go away. Wait a little longer, and natural healing will take its course. You will be emotionally and spiritually restored in the end."

Unfortunately, this is often not the case with emotional and spiritual wounds. Too often, we use the time-heals approach as an excuse to implement the do-nothing plan. Instead of dealing with our wounds, we ignore them. We hope the pain will subside or completely go away over time. Though the emotions may lessen or be pushed aside, time does not heal our wounds. Time does not make forgiveness easier or automatic. Over time, the wounds are covered over and pushed to the side. Left untreated, our hurt is allowed to fester, and over time, we slip into bitterness.

> it's important to recognize that time does not heal the wounds inflicted by hurtful deeds

Many of us have carried wounds since our childhood. Has time healed these wounds? Many would say no. There are so many men and women who still carry the burden of wounds they received as children. Time simply allows the wounds to take up residence. Eventually the bitterness takes hold of us. It infects our relationships and our marriages. Left unchecked, it can be passed on to our children and become a part of our legacy.

It's important to recognize that time does not heal the wounds inflicted by hurtful actions. We must choose to forgive even those offenses and wounds which occurred in our distant past. Contrary to common wisdom, forgiveness does not require the passage of time. Forgiveness allows God to give us true spiritual and emotional healing. Though forgiveness will not completely remove all emotions or consequences, we can trust God to be responsible for our emotional care and our future. We can trust God to bring true healing and remove the bitterness. Forgiveness is the surprising way to freedom!

FORGIVENESS MYTH #4: RECONCILIATION (IT TAKES TWO TO FORGIVE)

"I can't forgive my father for abusing me as a child! Every time I try to talk to him, he denies or downplays everything!" she said. Tammy felt like she was unable to escape her past. Her father's abusiveness still haunted her. She hated attending family reunions. Tammy had an underlying distrust of men. It was difficult for her to trust her own husband, even though he treated her with love and respect.

Tammy wanted to move past her childhood hurts. She saw how these experiences still harmed her and continued to damage her adult relationships, but she was stuck in a common misunderstanding about forgiveness. She believed she was unable to forgive her father until their relationship was reconciled. She believed that in order to forgive, she first needed to confront her father. If he would own up to his abusive behavior and ask her for forgiveness, then Tammy believed she would be able to forgive him. She was ready to be free from her past and move on with her life.

This misconstrued approach to forgiveness leaves many in a hopeless situation. Often perpetrators like Tammy's father have no intention of owning up to their offenses. I've worked with individuals who have been hurt by perpetrators who died long ago. If reconciliation were necessary for forgiveness, it would be impossible for these hurting individuals to ever find freedom. If forgiveness requires me to confront the bully who made my middle school years miserable, how am I supposed to find that person? Is my future peace and happiness dependent on meeting with the bully? This could be difficult or even impossible!

For others, it is inappropriate or even dangerous to approach the person who hurt them. Sometimes, the victim has no relationship with the perpetrator before the offense was committed. Would God require a rape victim to enter into a relationship with the rapist in order to experience reconciliation? Wouldn't this kind of personal contact put the victim in a very dangerous situation? This approach does not seem wise or appropriate.

Good news. It does not take two to forgive. Forgiveness is not dependent on reconciliation. We have the ability to forgive without ever interacting with the perpetrator. Forgiveness is a transaction which takes place between God and me. Forgiveness is simply giving God responsibility for the offense and the surrounding situation. Forgiveness is trusting God to bring justice to the offender.

In many situations it is appropriate and helpful to reconcile our relationships. Sometimes confronting others is important. Reconciliation can be an important part of bringing healing to all involved in the situation. But reconciliation is a separate process from forgiveness. God gives us a way to experience the freedom of forgiveness, even when reconciliation is inappropriate or impossible.

David's dearest friend was Saul's son, Jonathan (1 Samuel 18:1-4). When David realized Saul was trying to kill him, David fled for his life (1 Samuel 19-21). David did forgive Saul by giving God the responsibility of bringing Saul to justice (1 Samuel 26:9) but was never able to reconcile with him. Being in hiding and continually on the run was a hard way of life for David and his men. He was forced to leave his wife, Michal. He was never again able to spend time with his dear friend, Jonathan. David reached out to Saul on multiple occasions, demonstrating he was not Saul's enemy. But Saul decided David was a threat and continued to hunt him down. Reconciliation was

> forgiveness is **not** dependent on reconciliation. Forgiveness is a transaction between God and me

not possible. It would have been unwise and unsafe for David to return to the palace and attempt to reconcile his relationship with Saul. Surely the king would have murdered David.

LIVING AT PEACE

[18] If it is possible, as far as it depends on you, live at peace with everyone. [19] Do not take revenge, my dear friends, but leave room for God's wrath, for it is written: "It is mine to avenge; I will repay," says the Lord (Romans 12:18-19).

Though a restored relationship is desirable, there is a basic assumption in this passage that it is not always possible. We are to seek to be at peace with everyone, but it is not always possible or wise to restore relationships with our perpetrators. God wants us to forgive everyone. But remember, forgiveness simply means trusting God to bring justice and avenge us for the evil done against us. (verse 19)

Living at peace with everyone does not mean we need to be in relationship with everyone. Boundaries are often godly and necessary for us to remain safe and live emotionally healthy lives. Sometimes the wisest way to live at peace with a volatile person is to keep a safe distance! Forgiveness is not reconciliation. It only takes one person to forgive. It is a transaction between God and me alone. In many cases, God may also want us to reach out and restore the damaged relationship, but if we are unable to reconcile, we can still choose to trust God. He can and will make things right. We can choose to release ourselves from bitterness and find freedom through forgiveness.

> living at peace with everyone does not necessarily mean we need to be in relationship with everyone

When I explained this principle to Tammy, it gave her a new hope that she could find freedom from her father's abuse. We worked through a process which allowed her to forgive her father. She chose to trust that God understood the entire situation and could bring justice to everyone involved. Sadly, Tammy's father had already passed, so she was never able to reconcile with him. This act of forgiveness gave her a new freedom and provided a foundation which allowed her to begin to heal the other damaged relationships in her life. She began to trust her husband in a way she never thought possible. Both Tammy and her husband were surprised and grateful for how God used forgiveness to transform their relationship.

PART 4

THE HOW OF
FORGIVENESS

10

forgiveness:
learning a how

I HAVE BEEN LEADING short-term mission's trips to Poland for several years. We always give new team members some practical advice about the Polish culture before we travel. For example, a kiss on both cheeks used to be a common greeting between men in Eastern European churches. Midwesterners are a bit more stoic, with a handshake being our most intimate greeting. We warn our team members, "If you receive a Polish greeting, make sure you keep your head still!"

On one occasion, I saw the unfortunate results of ignoring this practical advice. One of the elders of a Polish church wanted to warmly greet his American guest, Phil. The elder grabbed Phil by both shoulders and went in to plant a great big kiss on his cheek. Unfortunately, Phil did not keep his head facing straight forward. Both Phil and the Elder leaned the same way and Phil got a great big smooch right on the lips! As you can imagine, both men stepped back abruptly with uncomfortable, startled looks on their faces. It took every ounce of willpower I had to keep myself from bursting into laughter!

Phil went oversees to build relationship with Poles and do ministry together. He thought he knew how to greet a Polish man, but when he practiced his idea of "how," the results were not all he hoped they would be.

We can have a similar outcome when we forgive others. As I have talked with individuals, this is a common area where people get lost. People believe forgiveness is important. They are good about explaining the reasons "why" they should forgive others. They encourage one another to forgive, but many do not have an effective method "how" to forgive. Some of us—though we fully intend to forgive—find we are still stuck in the painful emotions.

LEARNING A HOW

Through the first three sections of this book, we discussed how we get stuck in unforgiveness. We have seen the destructive impact unforgiveness has on us emotionally, spiritually, and physically. We explored how the enemy can deceive us into living out and repeating these destructive patterns. We understand the reasons why we should practice forgiveness, and how this can set us free.

In this next section, we will take a look at a way we can practice forgiveness. It is a method I have found to be extremely helpful in my own life. I've walked countless men and women through this method, and it has taught them how to practice biblical forgiveness and find lasting freedom.

But before we proceed, let me reiterate that there is not a single, best formula for practicing forgiveness. Forgiveness itself is not a method, nor is it a particular step-by-step process. Forgiveness is a *choice* and a *belief*. It is a *choice* to give God responsibility for the offense. It is a *belief* that God is trustworthy and able to take responsibility for the offense and make things right.

If you are someone who has already learned an effective way to practice forgiveness, Praise God! It is neither my goal nor my intent to try to convince you I have found the best way. If God has used forgiveness in your life to set you free, have confidence in this freedom! Nothing in this book can make you any freer than the forgiveness you have already chosen.

> **many who believe forgiveness is important, do not have an effective method for "how" to forgive**

For many who have experienced forgiveness, what works well in their own lives is often difficult to explain to others. My friend, Aaron, wanted to explain to his daughter that she needed to forgive her husband. Aaron practiced forgiveness for many years and knew it was the path out of bitterness and into freedom. After years of practice, the "how" became almost automatic for him. The ruts ran deep down the path to forgiveness. The path to forgiveness was so automatic for Aaron, he was having a hard time explaining it to his daughter. He could explain to her why forgiveness was the right path forward, but every attempt to explain how instead came out sounding more like a spiritual cliché or another reason why she should forgive her husband.

"You just need to give it to God…"

"You need to forgive your husband because…"

"If you don't forgive, then the bitterness will only hurt you..."

As a result, Aaron's daughter knew all the reasons why she should forgive her husband but didn't understand how to forgive him. She ended up feeling hopeless and all alone in her marriage problems. Aaron wanted to learn a method for how to practice forgiveness—not for himself—but to help his daughter.

Even if forgiveness is something we know how to do in our own lives, it can be very helpful to learn a method which can be explained to others. Let's look at a step-by-step of how to practice forgiveness. It is not the only way, but it is an effective way which is consistent with the biblical principles we are discussing in this book.

As you continue reading, chapters 11 – 15 include a section labeled "Practicing Forgiveness," which will walk you through each step. I strongly recommend you do not skip forward without taking time to develop a broader understanding of each step. Each chapter builds upon the previous and prepares you to practice forgiveness in a variety of situations.

As we repeatedly practice this process of forgiveness, what starts out as a discipline will become a habit. In a short time, we will find that forgiveness is a normal part of our relationship with God. With practice, forgiveness will become the natural choice.

Let's jump right into the "how," because the most life-changing part of this book starts on the next page...

11

state the offense

FORGIVENESS IS GIVING Jesus responsibility to make things right for an offense we have suffered. I have found it is extremely helpful to acknowledge how I was hurt or offended to Jesus in prayer. When we come to him and prayerfully recount how we were hurt and how it made us feel, it helps us accept that an offense truly has taken place. When we share with Jesus how we felt offended, he begins to clear away much of the fog. He cuts through the false forgiveness our enemy uses to deceive and hinder us from finding the path to freedom.

Stating the offense is important because it does not leave room for us to fall back into the old forgive-and-forget method. Stating the offense is being honest with ourselves that an offense has truly taken place. We are not making excuses nor minimizing how we have been hurt, but we are admitting to ourselves and professing to God that we truly have been offended, hurt, and/or damaged by someone else's actions.

It is not our job to determine whether the person is guilty or has sinned before God. We are choosing to forgive because we have been offended. That's it. Let's say, for example, I am driving through a snowstorm on my way to my son's basketball game. As I am sitting at a stop sign, another driver hits a patch of ice and slides into my rear bumper. I am not happy. Not only do I have to go through all the trouble of getting my car repaired, but I am going to miss most of my son's game.

Have I suffered an offense? Is it reasonable for me to be annoyed or even angry? Absolutely! My car has been damaged, I have been seriously inconvenienced, my body is sore from the jolt of the impact, and it wasn't my fault. I am a little angry and resentful.

> we state
> the offense
> to Jesus because
> we are forgiving
> and trusting him to
> bring justice

Does this mean the other driver is guilty of sin before God? Were they driving irresponsibly, or the victim of a patch of ice? I will probably never know, but even if I was sure it was truly an accident and out of everyone's control, this would not completely take away my irritation and resentment.

Fortunately, though, forgiveness is both possible and appropriate, regardless of whether the person holds any guilt in the situation. When I state the offense to God, this is not an act of vengeance. In fact, it is the opposite of vengeance. I state the offense to Jesus in order to tell him how I feel, and in doing so, I am taking the first step toward trusting him to bring the justice he judges to be appropriate.

Forgiving the person does not remove the offender from their legal or financial obligations. We should expect to proactively participate in the legal process—with integrity—as called upon by the law. If my car is hit by another driver, I should expect the driver or his insurance company to cover the cost of repairs and medical expenses. I may need to file claims, even take some legal action, but forgiveness allows me to give God responsibility for bringing justice. Forgiveness allows me to be free from the bitterness, anger, and resentment that will try to creep into my heart and bring even more pain and hurt.

So, when I state the offense to Jesus, the guilt or innocence of the offender is not important. I am simply telling Jesus—from my perspective—what happened and how it hurt me.

PRACTICING THE HOW

As we move forward, you will find it helpful to practice the forgiveness steps in each of the chapters of this section. Think of an offense you suffered at some point in your life. Selecting a minor offense will be the most helpful for the first time through. Once you read through and understand the entire process, feel free to go back and repeat it with a more significant offense in mind.

It is even okay if you have already forgiven the offense you select. Have one or two specific events or offenses in mind so you can practice as you read along. You may want to jot these offenses down for your own reference as you read through and practice the steps of forgiveness.

IT'S YOUR TURN...

practicing forgiveness: state the offense

Forgiveness is a process between you and Jesus. In the quiet of your own heart and mind, go to one of your favorite places. For me it is a beach in Hanalei Bay, Hawaii. For some, it is a garden or a park setting. For others, this may be a favorite space at home. You pick a place where you would like to spend time alone with Jesus.

In your heart and mind, notice that you are in this place. As you enter this place you also notice Jesus is present with you, the true Jesus of the Scriptures. He is the Creator who shares in all of God's attributes (John 1:1-2). He practices wrath (Romans 1:28; John 3:36) and justice (John 5:30; Acts 17:31) in a way that is consistent with His righteousness (Philippians 3:9). He is the God of love (1 John 4:8, 1 Corinthians 13:4-7), and wants to be our friend (John 15:15). He is the One who exemplifies all the fruit of the Spirit: "But the Holy Spirit produces this kind of fruit in our lives: love, joy, peace, patience, kindness, goodness, faithfulness, gentleness, and self-control" (Galatians 5:22-23a, NLT).

Everything about Jesus lines up with the fruit of the Spirit. Jesus' character is loving, joyful, kind, patient, peaceful, gentle, self-controlled, faithful, and good. Take a minute and think about each of these character traits. Think about how much we might smile and even laugh as we spend time with Jesus who is joyful.

What would it be like to notice how good or patient Jesus is toward us? We are surprised by how much he truly loves us and treats us with kindness. Though he is all-powerful, his peace and self-control make us feel safe and protected in his presence. Though God has absolute authority to rule over us, he always treats us as a good and faithful friend would.

Once you have spent some time processing Jesus' true character as it is described and exhibited in the Scriptures, you can begin the forgiveness process. The purpose of processing and understanding his true nature is simply to set the table for a prayer conversation with Jesus around forgiveness.

Now, let's practice forgiveness with the one specific offense you have selected or written down. While you are still in your favorite place with Jesus, state the offense or hurt. Tell him exactly how the person wronged you. Explain how it impacts you. Show Jesus how this makes you feel. Be honest. Take time to list the ways it has affected you, your life, and your relationships. Tell him how this wrong has impacted you emotionally, physically, or spiritually.

The purpose of this exercise is not to stir up anger, cast judgment, nor seek revenge. However, it is important for us to be honest with ourselves and with God that a real offense has taken place. If we cannot reconcile in our own hearts and minds that we have been wronged, we will be hindered in our ability to forgive the offense. Feeling the weight of the hurt will help us clarify exactly what we are *choosing* to forgive.

WANDA AND JEFF'S GAMBLING (PART 1)

Let's see how this step of stating the offense plays out in a real-life example. Wanda and Jeff had been married for fifteen years. Jeff was feeling bored with his life and career and began gambling online. Many people dabble in occasional gambling, but for Jeff, the pastime turned into an outright addiction. Sadly, he burned through most of the family's savings in a few short months.

Jeff got help with his addiction and was no longer gambling, but as I talked with Wanda, it quickly became apparent she was very bitter. She wanted to be able to trust Jeff again but felt like he stole away the financial security they had built together. She shared how the financial buffer was gone and how much she hated having to start over.

Jeff asked her for forgiveness, and Wanda chose to forgive him, but she admitted that every time she wanted to buy anything, she would get angry because she had to second-guess whether they could afford it. Their plans to remodel the kitchen had to be put on hold. Wanda doubted if the kitchen remodel would ever be possible. There was a lot of tension in their relationship, and she was emotionally exhausted.

I encouraged Wanda to forgive her husband and invited her to allow me to walk her through the forgiveness process.

She agreed. She wanted to try to forgive her husband. First, I encouraged her to "state the offense" directly to Jesus.

As she was standing before Jesus, she began in prayer, "Jesus, Jeff lied to me because he felt like he didn't have any other options."

She continued, "Jeff squandered all of our money away, because of his addiction and lack of control over his gambling."

I began to see a pattern in Wanda's prayers and quietly asked her to pause, saying, "I noticed with every accusation, you are giving Jeff an excuse. You are giving reasons to make his hurtful choices and behaviors seem reasonable or even justified. What is there to forgive if you don't really believe Jeff did anything wrong?"

Wanda was confused by this question at first. She was uncomfortable making these accusations directly to Jesus. She felt like making such strong statements against her husband was unkind—possibly even unchristian. This didn't seem like forgiving to her.

So, I asked, "Isn't it God's job to decide whether or not your husband was justified in these choices? Your job is only to be honest with yourself and with God about how Jeff hurt you. Let's try again. This time, simply state Jeff's offenses to Jesus without making any excuses for him."

Wanda agreed and decided to pray again, "Jesus, Jeff deceived me and lied over and over to hide his gambling habit. I feel betrayed. I feel like I can never trust Jeff again."

> God will not crush us under the weight of forgiveness. He knows how to bring healing with gentleness

She continued, "Jesus, Jeff squandered all of our money. I feel like all the hard work and years of saving have been stolen away from me. I resent Jeff because I always feel broke. If Jeff wouldn't have hidden the truth...if he wouldn't have lied to me over and over...we could have found help. We would have been able to stop the financial drain before all our money was gone!"

Wanda took her time and tearfully explained to Jesus the many ways Jeff hurt her. It was not a long, drawn-out process, but Wanda took enough time to be thorough. She prayed and asked Jesus if there were any other offenses she did not remember. He brought a couple of things to mind that Wanda had totally forgotten. She immediately saw the value of bringing these offenses to Jesus for forgiveness.

Our purpose was not to stir up anger or bitterness. Although Wanda felt some strong emotions, she understood that she needed to be open and transparent with Jesus. This enabled her to give responsibility for these offenses over to Jesus.

As we completed the rest of the steps through the forgiveness process, Wanda was amazed by the immediate freedom she began to experience. Of course, there were still financial difficulties ahead, but Wanda found she was able to love and respect her husband again. For the first time in years, Wanda and Jeff began to feel like they were truly partners working on the same team.

OPENING PANDORA'S BOX

"You want me to ask Jesus to reveal other offenses?"

Pamela bristled at the idea. She was suddenly worried; anxiety began to take hold. Pamela knew she needed to forgive her parents but had blocked out many of the horrible experiences surrounding her father's abuse. As a middle-aged adult, Pamela remembered little. Her father had spent years in prison, so she knew he must have done some terrible things to her or her brothers. She remembered the social workers showing up at her home. She remembered she told them *something* but blocked out the details. One thing was certain: Pamela had no desire to dredge up these potentially horrific memories of sexual abuse.

Pamela's concerns are understandable. Many of us have memories so stressful or terrible, we push them to the back of our mind or even forget them altogether. Do we really want to ask God to bring these awful things back to memory and suffer through them again?

In Matthew 11, Jesus was in Galilee preaching to a crowd when he said these words:

> [28]Then Jesus said, "Come to me, all of you who are weary and carry heavy burdens, and I will give you rest. [29]Take my yoke upon you. Let me teach you, because I am humble and gentle at heart, and you will find rest for your souls. [30]For my yoke is easy to bear, and the burden I give you is light" (Matthew 11:28-30, NLT).

With these words, Jesus gives us a wonderful glimpse into his character. Jesus wants to take away the burdens of unforgiveness. If we ask him for direction through the forgiveness process, he will not dump an even heavier burden upon us! His spirit is humble. He is gentle. Any burden he asks us to carry will feel easy and light. Jesus wants to teach us and show us the way to find rest for our souls.

I have seen this play out for many, many individuals. Jesus is trustworthy. If we ask Jesus for direction—and wait for answers from the Holy Spirit—we can trust God. God does not want to overwhelm us or crush us. He knows how to bring healing with gentleness.

As I watch God at work, some offenses are "no big deal" but still cause a debilitating bitterness. Others are too horrible to write about. That being said, I have never seen anyone crushed under the weight of the forgiveness process. Some remember just enough incidents to be able to state the offence accurately. Very few victims need to remember traumatic or abusive incidents in detail. Sometimes, God will only bring to memory a single situation, and there are often tears of sadness.

Fear is normal, but once the forgiveness process is complete, I often hear the words, "Wow, that wasn't so bad!"

Pamela needed a few minutes to process this. She was still afraid but decided to trust Jesus enough to ask him the question, "Ok, Jesus, are there any other offenses or situations you want to bring to my mind?"

Pamela was surprised, though she was confident God had given her clear direction. She told me, "I don't think God wants me to remember each situation. He only wants me to state all the abuse as one single offense. Jesus wants me to tell him how I feel this abuse affected me. It is not necessary to recount all the details."

Pamela was so relieved! She was able to complete the forgiveness process. As we closed the session, we prayed together, "Jesus, I ask you to be in charge of these memories. I trust them to your care and ask that you will never allow them to come back unless they can be helpful."

Pamela experienced God's healing power through forgiveness that day. To her surprise, the bitterness is gone, and she has reconciled her relationship with her parents. She put healthy boundaries in place and will never allow her children to be alone with her father, but God has shown her a new way forward with her entire family.

12

the box

"JUST GIVE IT TO JESUS."

If you grew up in a church the way I did, you probably heard this statement many times. However, I have discovered that many of us do not really know "how" to give something to Jesus. Of course, we agree wholeheartedly. We believe we should give our cares to Jesus. Often, people even say the right words, "I give this to you, Jesus." But as I talk with hurting individuals—I have found many do not know how to give their cares to Jesus in a way that seems real. Some do not even understand what they are asking Jesus to take from them. As a result, we experience mixed results at best. Many are left feeling more confused than they were before. *I gave this to Jesus! Why does it seem like it still follows me everywhere I go?*

I still remember the images depicting complex atoms from my high-school chemistry class. I analyzed the diagrams showing electrons passing straight through the crowded nucleus of protons and neutrons at the speed of light. I asked my teacher, "How is this possible? How do these electrons pass straight through this solid nucleus? Why don't these electrons smash into this pack of protons and neutrons?"

the box is a metaphor built in our thoughts, designed to help bring clarity to the forgiveness transaction

My teacher explained it to me this way: Physicists describe the structure of an atom through mathematical formulas. Chemistry is about understanding these formulas. The diagram is not an exact scientific representation of the atom. The formulas are the real science. Physicists draw the diagrams to help us wrap our minds around the physical properties of the atomic structure. Because our brains comprehend complex concepts better through pictures and stories, scientists have created these diagrams to help simplify and clarify these complex interactions. But the math accurately describes the interactions of sub-atomic particles, not the diagrams.

Jesus understood the importance of this principle. He was a master communicator. He often used metaphors, analogies, parables, and real-life examples to teach spiritual principles. Because Jesus understands how our brains work, he knows how these word-pictures give us a more complete understanding of spiritual truth. The metaphors help bring clarity and meaning. We connect with them—not only on an intellectual level—but also on a personal and emotional level.

Jesus even used these kinds of metaphors in his prayers. For example, in The Lord's Prayer, Jesus prays, "And forgive us our debts, as we also have forgiven our debtors" (Matthew 6:12). Is forgiveness a financial transaction? Do those who offend us owe a financial debt? Of course not! Jesus used this metaphor because he knew it would bring a much deeper understanding of injustice and forgiveness.

Forgiveness is giving responsibility for offenses to Jesus. "The Box" is a metaphor built in our thoughts, designed to help bring clarity to the forgiveness transaction which occurs between Jesus and me. It is a metaphor to help our minds process our prayerful conversations with Jesus and to interact with God in a way that solidifies the spiritual truths for us. It helps us to believe forgiveness has truly taken place.

IT'S YOUR TURN...

practicing forgiveness: the box

Some of you completed the steps as you read "Practicing Forgiveness: Stating the Offense" in Chapter 11. If you did so, I trust you were open and transparent with yourself (and before Jesus) about how you were hurt or offended by the person you are choosing to forgive. Now, let's step back into the metaphor we have created in our mind and continue with the next step in the forgiveness process.

As you proceed within this metaphor, you are still in your favorite place with Jesus. Notice there is an empty box. Now, put each of the offenses you stated to Jesus in this box. Feel the weight of each offense as you place it into the box. Again, take your time and place any offense the Holy Spirit brings to your mind into the box.

Continuing with the metaphor, tape up the box and seal it shut. Pick up the box and feel the weight of it as you hand it to Jesus. Feel the weight go as he takes it. Tell Jesus you are giving him full responsibility for these offenses. Tell him you no longer want to be responsible for bringing the offender to justice, but with this box, you are giving the responsibility to Jesus.

Helpful Notes:

1. **How do you put the offenses into the box?**

   Some people see a picture of the offense and put this picture into the box. Some write each offense on a piece of paper and put the paper into the box. Some see the title of the offense and put it into the box. Others simply have a sense they are putting each general issue into the box. There is no "right way." These are all metaphors, so do what works for you! The important thing is to find a way that connects for you, and—as you process each offense—put it into the empty box.

2. **Do the offenses seem too big for your box?**

   Sometimes you may want to use a very large box or even put the offenses in more than one box.

3. What if the offenses are so big the box seems too heavy or overwhelming for me to lift?
Ask Jesus to help you lift the box.

4. Does this mean I must give up all my legal rights?
Giving Jesus responsibility for an offense does not mean we give up our legal rights. If the offender has broken the law, it may be appropriate to prosecute or participate in the legal process *after* you have forgiven.

Remember, forgiveness is always *your* choice. The reason God calls you to forgive is because he wants you to experience freedom. No one is forcing you to put things in the box or to give them to Jesus. Forgiveness is a choice only you can make. If you choose not to forgive, God will allow you to strap offenses on your own back and continue to carry them with you as long as you wish.

WANDA AND JEFF'S GAMBLING (PART 2)

Let's return to Wanda and Jeff's story. In Chapter 11, Wanda told Jesus about Jeff's gambling addiction and the ways it affected her. She was confident Jesus heard her and understood how hurt and angry she felt when she discovered all their savings were gone. Now, she continued to process the metaphor of her favorite place with Jesus.

"Notice there is an empty box near you," I said. "As Jesus is with you, place each one of the offenses into the empty box."

I quietly waited. "Oh, boy," Wanda said after a little while, "I am running out of room in the box. I have a lot of big things to put in there!"

We laughed as I said, "Feel free to add more boxes if you need them."

When Wanda finished, I said, "Ask Jesus if there are any other offenses he wants you to put in the box."

A couple more things came to Wanda's mind, and she placed those items in the box too. When Wanda indicated that she was finished, I said, "Okay, close the box and seal it shut. Now, pick up the box. Tell Jesus you are giving him responsibility for Jeff's actions and for each offense. Tell him you are forgiving Jeff and choosing to trust God to be responsible for the consequences of Jeff's actions. Feel the weight of the box go as you hand it over to Jesus."

> if other people also offended us in this situation, it is important to bring these to Jesus as well

I waited as Wanda completed this process with Jesus. "Wow," she said, "when I was holding the box, it seemed so heavy, but when I gave it to Jesus, it was so light for him!"

"Yes," I agreed, "because these offenses are not too big for Jesus to handle! Notice that Jesus takes the box away to a place where he takes care of it. He is loving and wise enough to take care of each of these on your behalf."

FORGIVING OTHER OFFENDERS

"Was anyone else involved in this situation?" I asked Wanda.

Wanda looked a little bit confused. "What do you mean?" she

asked. "I already forgave Jeff for his gambling issues. I already put this situation in the box and Jesus took it away."

"Yes," I said, "But was there anyone else involved in this situation? Is there anyone else who knew or was enabling Jeff's gambling problem? Is there anyone else who you are upset with and need to forgive?"

Sometimes when we are hurt, we become so focused on the primary offender that we forget about the other people who are involved in the situation. Perhaps there was another person who encouraged the hurtful behavior, or someone in authority who chose not to step in and help.

If we are frustrated, upset, or even bitter towards other people who also offended us in this situation, it is important for us to bring these offenses to Jesus as well. Of course, many situations will only include a single offender. It is not helpful to invent offenses where none exist, but when there are others who need to be forgiven, it is important to put these offenses in the box too.

WANDA AND JEFF'S GAMBLING (PART 3)

Wanda couldn't think of anyone else who offended her in this situation, so I encouraged her to ask Jesus if there was anyone else he wanted her to forgive. After a short conversation with Jesus, Wanda said, "Jesus reminded me how angry I am with my in-laws. I went to Jeff's parents for help, but they did nothing. They made it clear to me they did not want to take sides or even talk about it."

Wanda prayerfully put each of her in-law's offenses into a new box. As she handed the box to Jesus, she chose to forgive Jeff's parents and give responsibility for these offenses to Jesus. As Jesus took the box away, Wanda felt the weight of her anger and bitterness go.

practicing forgiveness: other offenders

Let's take another look at the situation you are forgiving as you read through these chapters. Are there other offenders in the situation? If you are unsure, ask Jesus, "Is there anyone else in this situation you want me to forgive?"

Notice Jesus' response. If there is no one else to forgive, he may bring no offenses to mind or simply respond, "No." If there are other offenders in this situation, you can be confident God will bring these to mind (James 1:5-7). God's Spirit may bring a picture to mind which depicts an offense or person he wants you to forgive. He may respond verbally, giving you the name of another person to be forgiven. For some, the Holy Spirit may simply bring forward painful feelings of resentment hidden in your heart.

God wants you to be completely free! Jesus knows you intimately and loves you immeasurably. His Spirit will bring these things to mind the way that is most helpful to you. It may be painful to remember some of these offenses, but don't panic if you shed a few tears. Jesus is near you, ready to take these away and care for them from now on.

Now, notice a new box before you and explain each offense to Jesus. Tell him how each one impacted you and made you feel. When you have put each offense into the box, tape it up and seal it shut. Give the box to Jesus, feeling the weight of it go as Jesus takes it. Notice that Jesus takes the box away.

When Jesus returns, ask him again whether there is anyone else in this situation he would like you to forgive. Take your time and forgive each person. Continue giving new offenses and boxes to Jesus until he indicates there are no other offenders in this situation. Even if there are many boxes, your situation is not a burden for Jesus. God wants you to be completely free from the burden of resentment you've been carrying.

13

confession

³ Why do you look at the speck of sawdust in your
brother's eye and pay no attention to the plank in your
own eye? ⁴ How can you say to your brother, 'Let me
take the speck out of your eye,' when all the time there
is a plank in your own eye? ⁵ You hypocrite, first take
the plank out of your own eye, and then you will see
clearly to remove the speck from your brother's eye
(Matthew 7:3-5).

It is difficult for me to picture this parable without laughing. Let
me describe what I see in my overactive imagination. I picture a guy,
with a long two-by-four board literally protruding from his eye socket.
Completely oblivious, he walks into a fine crystal store. Browsing over
the delicate crystal stemware and fine china, he is unaware of the plank
wildly swinging around the store with each turn of his head. Entire
shelves full of Waterford, Swarovski, and Lenox are demolished as
shards are sent flying in every direction.

This one-man wrecking ball approaches the back counter as the sounds of broken porcelain and crystal slowly settle around him. The store clerk looks around in wide-eyed horror as the room is filled with a deafening silence. The man leans in, tilting his head just right to see the clerk with his one good eye and insists, "Son, let me help you there. I see you've got a speck of dust in your eye!"

Though this is probably not the exact story Jesus told, I am pretty sure there was some snickering in the crowd as Jesus made this statement. When we are living in the fog of bitterness, we are all in danger of being unable to recognize the "plank in our own eye." Bitterness can cloud our ability to see where we have made unwise decisions or actions which have been hurtful to others.

God's forgiveness is just

In many situations when we have been offended, we may carry some guilt for our own actions as well. We need to take responsibility for our part and ask God's forgiveness for any sins we committed. In Jesus' words, "we need to take the plank out of our own eye" (Matthew 7:5).

In our bitterness, we often cannot see our own offenses. Even when our guilt is a real part of the situation, bitterness makes it difficult to see beyond our own anger and hurt. Of course, in some situations we may not have sinned. We may have responded in a godly way. But often, we are unable to even consider whether we hold responsibility for some of our own inappropriate behaviors and actions until after we have released our resentment toward other offenders.

This is the reason it is helpful to forgive others first, before we consider whether we need to confess any part in the situation and ask forgiveness. As we release anger and resentment towards others—once the fog of bitterness begins to clear—it will be easier to take a step back and have a much more accurate view of the entire situation. Only then can we be confident our minds are cleared to objectively answer the question: do I need to ask for God's forgiveness for any part I played in this situation?

WILL GOD FORGIVE ME EVEN THOUGH I...?

The apostle John wrote, "⁹If we confess our sins, he is faithful and just and will forgive us our sins and purify us from all unrighteousness" (1 John 1:9).

The important principle is this: God asks us to take responsibility for our sins. Jesus is ready to forgive, but he takes away our sins only when we first take responsibility for them. When we confess our sins to God, we are simply agreeing with him that we are guilty and in need of forgiveness.

Jesus' forgiveness is not only an act of mercy and grace, but John also points out that God's forgiveness is *just*. When Jesus forgives us, he is taking responsibility to carry out the justice. In fact, justice has already been carried out by Jesus on the cross. He took the punishment for our sins when he died for us. The hard part is already done! We only need to confess our sins and accept God's forgiveness!

Like the other steps in the forgiveness process, the purpose of confession is to find freedom. God does not want to shame us or beat us up emotionally. Jesus has already made the difficult sacrifice, dying to provide forgiveness for our sins (Romans 5:8, John 3:16-18).

God desires for us to live free and to enjoy a restored relationship with him. In this step, we are taking responsibility for anything wrong or inappropriate we may have done in the situation.

Of course, in many cases, the victim has no responsibility. For example, when a child has been mistreated or abused by an authority figure, the child seldom has any responsibility. Let's not invent areas of guilt so we can check off a step. However, it is important to at least ask Jesus if there is anything we need to confess. Then, if he brings anything to mind, we can complete this process.

After we forgive others, the Holy Spirit will make us aware of sin we need to confess and receive forgiveness for. David prayed:

> [23] Search me, God, and know my heart;
>   test me and know my anxious thoughts.
> [24] See if there is any offensive way in me,
>   and lead me in the way everlasting
>   (Psalm 139:23-24).

David's prayer is appropriate for us to practice, even when we have been hurt. God wants to have a restored relationship with us.

IT'S YOUR TURN...

practicing forgiveness: confession

If you are practicing the forgiveness process with your own situation, in the past few chapters you forgave the offender and anyone else who Jesus brought to mind. Take a moment to step back into the metaphor. Notice you are in your favorite place, and Jesus is there with you. Are you aware of anything in this situation you need to confess? If nothing comes to mind, ask Jesus if there is anything you need to confess to him and expect. As you ask, expect Jesus to answer.

As you listen for an answer, Jesus will often bring something to mind. He uses pictures, words, or feelings to reveal these to us. If God says, "No," or nothing to confess is brought to mind, then this step is completed. Thank Jesus for helping you.

If Jesus did bring something to mind, though, continue on with this step. Within the metaphor, notice there is another empty box. Tell Jesus openly and honestly about each of the things which came to mind. Confess to him that what you did was wrong. As you confess each sin, put it into the box.

Once again, take enough time to be thorough. Ask Jesus whether there is anything else you need to confess. Tape up your box and seal it shut. Pick up the box and feel the weight of it as you hand it to Jesus. Feel the weight go as he takes it. Tell Jesus you are giving him full responsibility for your offenses. Tell Jesus you are accepting his forgiveness as he takes this box from you.

Thank Jesus for answering your prayers. Take as much time as you would like to give thanks for his forgiveness, healing, and love.

WANDA AND JEFF'S GAMBLING (PART 4)

"I guess I was pretty hard on Jeff. I said some things to him that were not very kind. In my frustration and anger, I told him, 'I wish I never met you! If it wasn't for the kids, I would have left you a long time ago!'"

When Wanda asked Jesus whether there was anything she needed to confess, there were a few offenses which came to mind. "Tell Jesus about the way you treated Jeff and the things you said to him. Place each item into a new, empty box."

Wanda was still with Jesus, and she prayed these words directly to him, "Jesus, I confess I said some unkind things to Jeff. I told him I wished I had never met him. I told Jeff that—if it weren't for the kids—I would have left him a long time ago. I was angry and made these statements because I wanted to hurt Jeff. I was wrong to treat Jeff in this way."

When Wanda indicated that she was finished, I suggested, "Ask Jesus if there is anything else you need to confess."

For the next few minutes, Wanda waited as Jesus brought forward a few things that she was guilty of in the situation. She confessed each of these to Jesus and put each one into the metaphorical box. She sealed up the box and handed it to Jesus. As Jesus took the box, she felt the weight go with it. "Jesus, I accept your forgiveness. Thank you for taking my sins on the cross. Thank you for restoring my relationship with God."

14

boxing up self-judgment

"IF GOD HAS FORGIVEN ME, why do I still feel so guilty?" After seeing the amazing changes in Wanda, Jeff came in by himself to see me. Together, Jeff and I worked through his forgiveness process. But even after he confessed his offenses and accepted Jesus' forgiveness, Jeff felt like he was still carrying a heavy load of guilt and pain. He said, "If God has forgiven me—and I do believe he has—why do I still feel so guilty?"

"Have you forgiven *yourself* for your gambling?" I asked.

Jeff looked dumbfounded, "I already asked Jesus to forgive me, and I accepted his forgiveness. What do you mean, 'Do I forgive myself?' I am not sure I want to forgive myself. I want to make sure I never do this again!"

So, I asked Jeff, "You asked Jesus to forgive you. You accepted his forgiveness, right?"

"Right," he said.

"Well, do you think it is reasonable hold yourself to higher standards than Jesus does?"

"What do you mean?" Jeff asked.

"Well, it was reasonable for Jesus to forgive you. You accepted it. If you are unwilling or unable to forgive yourself, aren't you holding yourself to a higher standard than God's standard?

"Remember, forgiving is not forgetting. It is important to put accountability in place in order to keep you from falling into these behaviors in the future. Self-forgiveness simply means you no longer need to beat yourself up for your past sins. It means releasing yourself from self-judgment and giving responsibility over to God."

It wasn't easy for Jeff, but after processing this for several minutes, he decided to forgive himself.

SELF-FORGIVENESS

For many of us, accepting Jesus' forgiveness is easier than forgiving ourselves or even forgiving others. We may believe that if we forgive ourselves, then we are giving ourselves permission to repeat the bad behaviors. If we hold onto enough shame and maintain a steady dose of consequences, then we believe we will be motivated to stay away from repeating the bad behavior.

As we learned in Chapter 7, withholding forgiveness from ourselves is the opposite of what the Bible teaches. When we judge ourselves in this way, we continue to be stuck in bitterness. The bitterness boomerang will cause this self-judgment to be aimed outward. In this state of mind, we cannot help but also judge the people around us. Our minds remain trapped in the fog of bitterness. Until we choose to show mercy toward ourselves, we will continue to make poor choices, which will hurt ourselves and all within our sphere of influence.

KARA

I worked with Kara, a single woman who was struggling with self-forgiveness. Though she was a charming young lady, Kara avoided dating because of inappropriate choices she made in her teen years. She forgave the young men she had dated for their part in the situation. She also confessed and accepted God's forgiveness. But Kara believed she needed to continue to punish herself and, therefore, avoided any and all meaningful relationships. She immersed herself in her career and ministry. Stuck in the fog, Kara accepted her self-imposed loneliness and remained single for years. The bitterness boomerang effect was present as the self-judgment was also aimed outward toward others. She held men in judgment, with a core belief that they all would want to push her boundaries of physical intimacy.

> self-forgiveness is releasing myself from self-judgement and giving responsibility over to God

As we talked, Kara realized how she was harboring self-bitterness. She began to see how this was impacting her life and fueling the way she judged anyone around her who was dating. She recognized how important it was to forgive herself and worked through this process with Jesus. As she handed the box to Jesus, she couldn't believe how heavy it was!

With a newfound freedom, Kara began to allow herself to date again. She found trustworthy people to keep her accountable to remain pure in her dating relationships. Once the fog of self-bitterness was lifted, Kara found she was free to pursue her goal of marriage by dating

Christian men—without abandoning her pre-marriage boundaries for physical intimacy.

We know it is important to forgive others. We know it is important to confess our own sins and accept God's forgiveness. But we must also choose to forgive ourselves so we can live fully in the freedom God wants for us.

IT'S YOUR TURN...

practicing forgiveness: boxing up self-judgment

This section will give you an opportunity to continue to practice the self-forgiveness steps with your own situation. Now, return to your favorite place with Jesus. Ask him if there is anything you need to forgive yourself for. What are the things you hold against yourself? Does the Holy Spirit bring anything to mind? If so, notice a new box and explain each to Jesus as you put it into the box.

Once again, take enough time to be thorough. Ask Jesus whether there is anything else you need to forgive yourself for. He may let you know there is nothing else he wants you to deal with for now. Whatever the Holy Spirit brings to mind, put it into the box.

When you finish putting items in the box, tape it up and seal it shut. Pick up the box and feel the weight of it. Hand the box over to Jesus. Feel the weight go as he takes it. Tell Jesus you will no longer beat yourself up or try to bring yourself to justice. Tell Jesus you give him full responsibility for your offenses.

WANDA AND JEFF'S GAMBLING (CONCLUSION)

After Jeff worked through the forgiveness process for himself, the change in their relationship was astounding. Self-forgiveness allowed the marriage to continue to heal. They were on the road to reconciliation—and it took a lot of work and perseverance! Jeff had to earn back Wanda's trust over time. He developed accountability relationships to help protect him from getting pulled back into gambling. They both knew they had a long road ahead to rebuild their financial stability.

For Wanda and Jeff, forgiveness gave them both a new sense of freedom. It provided a foundation which allowed for continued healing. With God's help, they rebuilt their trust and love for one another. It was beautiful to watch this unfold.

15

thankfulness: sealing the deal

the story of Jesus and the ten lepers:

> [11] Now on his way to Jerusalem, Jesus traveled along the border between Samaria and Galilee. [12] As he was going into a village, ten men who had leprosy met him. They stood at a distance [13] and called out in a loud voice, "Jesus, Master, have pity on us!"
>
> [14] When he saw them, he said, "Go, show yourselves to the priests." And as they went, they were cleansed.
>
> [15] One of them, when he saw he was healed, came back, praising God in a loud voice. [16] He threw himself at Jesus' feet and thanked him—and he was a Samaritan.

[17] Jesus asked, "Were not all ten cleansed? Where are the other nine? [18] Has no one returned to give praise to God except this foreigner?" [19] Then he said to him, "Rise and go; your faith has made you well" (Luke 17:11-19).

Under Old Testament law, the unclean were forced to live outside of town so they would not infect anyone else. When they encountered people, they were required to hold their hand over their mouth and cry out, "Unclean! Unclean!" They were required to wear torn clothes and were not allowed to shave or cut their hair (Leviticus 13:45-46). Today, we would probably call this the "grunge" or "hippy" look and not take much notice. But in Jesus' day, these men were truly outcasts. No one was allowed to intermingle with them, and their appearance was so shocking, people avoided them. So when they saw Jesus, they yelled out from a distance, "Jesus, Master, have pity on us!"

Jesus saw the men and had compassion on them. He immediately asked them to go and show themselves to the priests, who were considered qualified to pronounce a person free of leprosy (Leviticus 13:2-3). The passage doesn't tell us what was going on in the minds of the lepers, but I suspect they were uncertain and even disappointed. They heard Jesus' instructions, but the leprosy was still clearly visible. They were not healed but decided to follow Jesus' instructions anyway.

As they made their way to the priest, the leprosy miraculously cleared from their skin, and they were healed. Nine of the ten men proceeded directly to the priest. Maybe they were eager to see their loved ones? Perhaps they were anxious to get their jobs and their lives back in order? Whatever the reason, it seems they quickly returned to the lives they knew prior to the leprosy.

But the tenth man, a Samaritan, decided to come back. The passage says he made a lot of noise praising God as he came back to find Jesus. He must have made quite a spectacle of himself! This straggly-haired Samaritan, with torn and tattered clothes, was walking down the road loudly blurting out praises of thanks and gratitude to God. I suspect other travelers gave him plenty of space. But instead of toning things down as he approached Jesus, the Samaritan went in head-first. He literally prostrated himself on the dirt, grabbed Jesus by the feet, and thanked him for healing his leprous skin.

I would guess the disciples took a step back as this seemingly crazed individual approached. Jesus saw the sincerity of the man's actions and was drawn to him. He accepted the Samaritan's thanks and commended his gratitude. As he sent the man on his way, Jesus said to him, "your faith has made you well" (Luke 17:19).

All ten men had enough faith to go and show themselves to the priests. All ten men decided to obey Jesus even though they still had the disease. This was a big step of faith for all! But the Samaritan came back to Jesus and gave thanks. Is Jesus changing the subject from "being thankful" to "having faith?" Or is it possible there is a relationship between thankfulness and faith?

ATTITUDE OF GRATITUDE?

Perhaps you have heard the slogan, "attitude of gratitude." The idea behind this phrase is that if our attitude includes gratefulness, then thanksgiving will naturally flow from us. But first we should ask whether thankfulness is an attitude or a practice?

An *attitude* is something we feel. It happens in our hearts and minds in a way that changes our actions. We may be able to choose or change an attitude, but it generally happens internally before it affects our outward expressions and actions. For example, when our attitude is "angry," our words and actions often display this anger outwardly. When our attitude is "joyful," we can hardly help but show this joy on our faces and in our mannerisms.

A *practice* on the other hand is something we simply choose to do. For example, we may practice goodness by doing good things for others. We may not feel like doing good, but it's an action we choose. We may feel at any given moment like being selfish, but regardless of our feelings, we may still choose to practice acts of goodness toward other people.

So, which best describes thankfulness? Attitude or practice?

The easy and clear answer is both! There are times when we feel gratefulness so deeply it overflows naturally from our hearts in words of thanksgiving and praise. But it is interesting that Scripture rarely asks us to "feel grateful" or "have an attitude of thankfulness." Instead, the word "thanks" almost always follows the word "give" in Scripture.

> **"Give thanks** in all circumstances; for this is God's will for you in Christ Jesus" (1 Thessalonians 5:18).

> **"Give thanks** to the Lord, for he is good" (Psalm 107:1a).

> "And whatever you do, whether in word or deed, do it all in the name of the Lord Jesus, **giving thanks** to God the Father through him" (Colossians 3:17)

> "And **give thanks** for everything to God the Father in the name of our Lord Jesus Christ" (Ephesians 5:20, NLT).

"that my glory may sing your praise and not be silent.
O Lord my God, I will **give thanks** to you forever!"
(Psalm 30:12, ESV)

When we read Scripture, we notice the words "thanks" and "thankful" are nearly always part of an action verb phrase. It is about giving thanks, offering sacrifices of thanksgiving, or singing praises of thanksgiving. It seems the kind of thanksgiving God is looking for is the *practice* of thanksgiving.

To me this is so important, because I don't believe God wants us to pretend to feel something in our hearts which is not genuine. This kind of false exterior was one of the reasons Jesus rejected the "religion" of the Pharisees. They were good at pretending to be holy and saying the right things, but it was all just an act so the Pharisees could hide the way they really felt in their hearts (Matthew 23:25-26).

Practice is different. It is something we do regardless of how we feel. We don't need to pretend to feel thankful. We are simply asked to practice thankfulness. While this difference may seem subtle, it has a huge impact on the way we approach gratitude.

> God asks us to **give** thanks in all situations, not to **feel** thankful in all situations

God asks us to "give thanks in all circumstances" (1 Thessalonians 5:18). Certainly, this includes undesirable circumstances, but does God want me to pretend to have an "attitude of gratitude" when I am clearly not feeling thankful? Should I pretend to feel thankful when

I just lost my job? What about when I have been betrayed or hurt? What if a loved one dies unexpectedly? Doesn't this seem awful, fake, and pretentious? These are all good and fair questions.

A few years ago, a close friend's marriage was falling apart. The divorce was nearly finalized. I was good friends with both the husband and the wife, and I was hurting for them. I shared their situation as a prayer request in my Bible study group. One well-meaning woman piped in, "Well, we should still be grateful because God..."

I don't remember the rest of the sentence. Her words sounded spiritual to me, but I felt hurt and a little angry. Should I be grateful my dear friends' marriage is falling apart? Should I feel grateful their kids will not have two parents in the home? No matter how I processed this divorce, I could not conjure up any true feelings of gratefulness.

thankfulness reinforces our faith in God's forgiveness

God asks us to *give* thanks in all situations, not to *feel* thankful in all situations. He wants us to notice things we can be thankful for and let God know we have noticed them. He does not ask us to pretend to feel grateful. He simply asks us to practice by giving thanks, in spite of the fact we don't always feel grateful on the inside. Feelings of gratefulness will often follow when we first choose to give thanks.

In any situation, there are many blessings we can find. I don't think God wants us to feel grateful for a divorce, but I found that I could express thanks for my friendship with this couple, for their awesome kids who are good friends with my kids, for the fun times our families have spent together, and for God's promise to walk through this difficult transition with them. Practicing thankfulness simply means choosing to notice the blessings and giving thanks to God.

THANKFULNESS AND FAITH

It turns out, there is a strong relationship between faith and giving thanks. When Jesus noted the Samaritan leper's thankfulness, he immediately followed up with the statement, "Your faith has made you well" (Luke 17:19). Due to the way our brain processes information, when we practice thankfulness, it solidifies our faith.

For example, we may ask God to forgive us for our sins. But for many of us, making such a request of God feels like only half of a conversation. I asked God to forgive my sins. How do I know if God heard my prayer? How do I know his answer? I know God promises to forgive me, but how can I be sure he has?

For most of us, these kinds of nagging questions remain just below the surface. As a result, we do the irrational—like asking God to forgive us for the same situation over and over again. Though we know God promises to forgive, this nagging doubt leaves us wondering whether God still holds the sin over our heads.

Asking God for forgiveness is only one example. God promises to supply all our needs (Matthew 6:25-34), but how often do we tell God we trust him and then continue to worry about our financial needs? God tells us he is trustworthy with our problems and anxieties (Philippians 4:6). How often do we ask God to help us and then immediately continue to worry? God has given us many promises. Though we say we believe these promises, it can be difficult for our brains to experience the kind of faith which brings about a change of thinking and behavior.

I believe this is why God asks us to *practice* thankfulness. When we thank God for keeping one of his promises, this sends a message to our own mind that the promise has already been kept. For example, when we ask God for forgiveness and then thank him for his forgiveness, this sends a vital message to our brains. The act of giving thanks not only solidifies the truth that God forgives, but our minds also benefit from the concrete action of accepting the forgiveness. This all reinforces our faith in God's forgiveness. It is done.

When we thank God for forgiving us, we are acknowledging receipt. This is a powerful reinforcement of our faith. Perhaps this is one of the truths Jesus was alluding to when he told the Samaritan, "Your faith has made you well." Jesus knew the Samaritan—by returning and giving thanks—was fully accepting the gift of healing. It solidified his faith.

THANKFULNESS AND FORGIVENESS

God wants us to fully experience his joy, peace, and freedom. This is only possible when we practice forgiveness and completely release the offenses we carry. When we give thanks, it strengthens our faith and completes the transaction in our minds.

Of course, God deserves our gratitude. He is pleased when we show appreciation for his extraordinary grace. But thankfulness also benefits us. Without it, doubt may creep back into our minds. I never skip the step of giving thanks when leading others through forgiveness. It is so important to thank Jesus each time he takes away the weight of the box we have been hauling around.

16

charting the course

THE PREVIOUS FIVE CHAPTERS demonstrated *how* to practice biblical forgiveness. This chapter will help to develop a broader understanding of this process. You may be reading this book for yourself, to find personal freedom that comes from forgiveness. You may be reading to learn tools of forgiveness in order to help bring others to freedom. This chapter is designed to chart this process which can be applied to most of the situations and offenses life brings our way.

Included are step-by-step instructions through the forgiveness process, organized as checklists. Each checklist walks you through part of the forgiveness process.

THE 10,000-FOOT VIEW

Before we dig into the checklists, let's look at the overall process at a high level. It can be divided into the following three parts:

FORGIVENESS PROCESS

A. Forgive the Offender (see Chapters 11, 12)

B. Forgive Others Involved (see Chapter 12)

C. Confession and Self-Forgiveness (see Chapters 13, 14)

Each of these names an important part of the forgiveness process. The step-by-step checklist for each of these is outlined in the following pages of this chapter.

Often, in order for an individual to find freedom, it is important to complete steps A, B, and C, as listed above. As we allow God's Spirit to lead this process, though, we will find that not all steps are needed in every situation.

It is also important to note—this forgiveness process is not a solution to every emotional or spiritual problem we might encounter. This book is not a comprehensive manual in biblical counseling, nor does it cover every scenario. It is focused on helping to resolve a single yet significant issue: unforgiveness. All of us will need to practice forgiveness many times in our lives, but not every issue we face can be resolved by practicing forgiveness. Forgiveness is a powerful tool provided by God to bring hope and freedom when we are stuck in unforgiveness.

PRACTICING

Some reading this book are looking for a way out of personal pain and disappointment. Others may be hoping to help a friend or loved one stuck in unforgiveness. Perhaps you are a minster, counselor, or a professional therapist. Regardless of background or training, it is important for each of us to practice forgiveness in our own lives before we lead others through this process. It is essential for us to first receive the healing we need for ourselves. We must apply the tools personally before trying to help others. As we experience the power of forgiveness in our own lives, we will be better equipped to help others.

So, whether you want to understand a way to do forgiveness for yourself or hope to be able to help others, it is important to dive into the process and practice it in your own life.

HOW TO USE THESE CHECKLISTS

The three checklists in this chapter provide a step-by-step guide to walking through this forgiveness process. It is designed to be as simple as possible, yet complete enough to apply to a wide range of situations.

This chart was developed by Equip2Counsel™ based on experience working through the forgiveness process one-on-one with hundreds of people. As an organization, we have been following this process and have found it to be broad enough to handle many of the most difficult situations, yet it is simple enough to help individuals forgive even the smallest offenses.

Of course, this is not the only way to practice forgiveness, but this process outlines a very clear methodology. I have found that completing these steps in order avoids many pitfalls which can cause an individual to become confused or stuck. It clearly leads people to a path of forgiveness and freedom. Feel free to review chapters 11-15 at any time for full instructions and examples demonstrating how to complete each step.

I recommend each of the three checklists be completed for every situation. Though not all steps are necessary for every situation, these checklists include instructions indicating when it is appropriate to skip steps. Completing each will allow God to call to mind all the things which need to be included in the forgiveness process. God wants us to be fully free of the resentment and bitterness that pulls us back into these hurtful situations and feelings. Completing each checklist will help to bring light to the dark corners of each offense. Don't worry, God will reveal what needs to be addressed for each situation so we can experience the peace and freedom he promises us.

> once we experience
> the power of
> forgiveness in our
> own lives, we will be
> better equipped
> to help others

A. FORGIVE THE OFFENDER

| Meet with Jesus | In the quiet of your heart and mind, notice that you are in a favorite place and Jesus is with you. |

1. state the offense

| Tell Jesus each offense and how it has affected you | Remember you are the prosecuting attorney, not the defense attorney. Jesus has perfect knowledge of all sides and whether any sin was actually committed. You are allowing him to be the Judge. |

2. the box

| Notice there is a box next to you | Most people choose a simple moving-size, cardboard box. |
| Place each offense in a box | You may put everything in the same box or use multiple boxes if one seems too full. |

3. giving the box to Jesus

Seal each box shut	
Pick up each box and feel the weight of the full box	If the box is too heavy, ask Jesus to help you pick it up.
Give each box to Jesus	As you give the box to Jesus, tell him you are giving him responsibility for the things in the box. Tell Jesus you are choosing to forgive the offender. Feel the weight of it go as he takes it away. It is now his responsibility.
Ask Jesus if there are any other offenses you need to forgive this person for	Ask and notice what offenses come to mind.
For any additional offenses brought to mind, start again with "Step 1. State the Offense"	Continue to repeat steps 1 through 3 until no other offenses come to mind for this person. Don't get discouraged if God brings many things to mind and you need to repeat these steps several times. God wants you to be free.

4. thankfulness

| Thank Jesus | Thank Jesus for making forgiveness possible through his death on the cross. Thank him for giving you freedom. |

B. FORGIVE OTHERS INVOLVED

Remember you are with Jesus	In the quiet of your heart and mind, notice that you are in a favorite place and Jesus is with you.
Ask Jesus if there is anyone else involved in this situation who you need to forgive	If others who you need to forgive come to mind, follow these steps to forgive each person involved in the situation. If no one comes to mind, proceed to "C. Self-Forgiveness."

1. state the offense

Tell Jesus each offense and how it has affected you	Remember you are the prosecuting attorney, not the defense attorney. Jesus has perfect knowledge of all sides and whether any sin was actually committed. You are allowing him to be the Judge.

2. the box

Notice there is a box next to you	Most people choose a simple moving-size, cardboard box.
Place each offense in a box	You may put everything in the same box or use multiple boxes if one seems too full.

3. giving the box to Jesus

Seal each box shut	
Pick up each box and feel the weight of the full box	If the box is too heavy, ask Jesus to help you pick it up.
Give each box to Jesus	As you give the box to Jesus, tell him you are giving him responsibility for the things in the box. Tell Jesus you are choosing to forgive the offender. Feel the weight of it go as he takes it away. It is now his responsibility.
Ask Jesus if there are any other offenses you need to forgive this person for	Ask and notice what offenses come to mind.
For any additional offenses brought to mind, start again with "step 1. state the offense"	Continue to repeat steps 1 through 3 until no other offenses come to mind for this person. Don't get discouraged if God brings many things to mind and you need to repeat these steps several times. God wants you to be free.

4. anyone else involved?

Ask Jesus if there is anyone else involved in the situation who you need to forgive	Ask and notice what offenses come to mind.
For any additional people brought to mind, start again with "step 1. state the offense"	Repeat steps 1 through 4 until no one else comes to mind.

5. thankfulness

Thank Jesus	Thank Jesus for making forgiveness possible through his death on the cross. Thank him for giving you freedom.

Remember you are with Jesus	In the quiet of your heart and mind, notice that you are in a favorite place and Jesus is with you.
Ask Jesus if there is anything you need to confess	If anything comes to mind you need to confess, follow these steps to ask God for forgiveness and to forgive yourself.
	If nothing comes to mind that you need to confess, skip these steps.

1. state the offense

Tell Jesus each offense and how it has affected you or hurt someone else	Remember you are the prosecuting attorney, not the defense attorney. Jesus has perfect knowledge of whether or not you actually sinned. We are allowing him to be the Judge.

2. the box

Notice there is a box next to you	Most people choose a simple moving-size, cardboard box.
Place each offense in a box	You may put everything in the same box or use multiple boxes if one seems too full.

3. giving the box to Jesus

Seal each box shut	
Pick up each box and feel the weight of the full box	If the box is too heavy, ask Jesus to help you pick it up.
Give each box to Jesus	As you give the box to Jesus, tell him you are giving him responsibility for the things in the box. Tell Jesus you are choosing to forgive the offender. Feel the weight of it go as he takes it away. It is now his responsibility.
Ask Jesus if there are any other offenses you need to confess	Ask and notice what offenses come to mind.
For any additional offenses brought to mind, start again with "step 1. state the offense"	Continue to repeat steps 1 through 3 until no other offenses come to mind.
	Don't get discouraged if God brings many things to mind and you need to repeat these steps several times. God wants you to be free.

4. thankfulness

Thank Jesus	Thank Jesus for making forgiveness possible through his death on the cross. Thank him for forgiving your offenses and for giving you freedom. (I John 1:9).

PART 5

FORGIVENESS
IN LIFE'S TOUGHEST
SITUATIONS

17

getting help from others

FORGIVENESS AND THE BODY OF CHRIST

Kimberly was hurting and confused. "I have been practicing the forgiveness process you taught me last week. It was helpful for a while, but it isn't working anymore."

"How so?" I asked.

"Well, Jesus won't take the box. In fact, I feel like he is avoiding me." She continued to explain that "Jesus would not forgive" her for a sexual relationship with a young man in her college years. "I guess this sin of sexual immorality is too big for God to just forgive."

Kimberly felt stuck as she sat in my office. She was convinced this particular sin was so great, it was not forgivable. She concluded that God wanted her to suffer—at least a little longer—for this sinful action.

But being outside of the situation, it was easy for me to identify and recognize these ideas as lies. As the Holy Spirit guided our conversation, she came to understand Jesus will never avoid us because it is outside of his character to do so (Deuteronomy 31:6-8). God's love and forgiveness is not based on our performance but on his own character of grace and mercy (Romans 5:8). Kimberly began to realize she was the one avoiding Jesus, because she believed the lie that her sin was unforgivable.

> when it comes to life's most difficult issues, we may need others to walk alongside us

All of us are deceived by the enemy at times in our lives. We get caught in common traps. We think to ourselves, *I need to get alone and hear from God on this.* And without any outside perspective, Satan's lies can seem completely reasonable.

But when it comes to life's most difficult issues, we may need others to walk alongside us and help bring us to healing. It is not God's plan for us to do life in isolation. In 1 Corinthians 12, Paul uses the metaphor "the Body of Christ" to explain the importance of living life in fellowship with other followers of Jesus.

1 Corinthians 12:21 says, "The eye can never say to the hand, 'I don't need you.' The head can't say to the feet, 'I don't need you.'"

God has designed each of us to function better in community. For us to achieve our God-given potential individually, we must learn to depend on one another. Solomon observed this truth in Ecclesiastes 4:12 as he talked about the importance of doing life in relationship with others: "Though one may be overpowered, two can defend themselves. A cord of three strands is not quickly broken."

Isolation is part of the enemy's strategy. He knows we are so much easier to deceive and overpower if we fight these battles on our own—without the wisdom and counsel of others within the Body of Christ. Solomon's principle applies to all kinds of difficulties, including the danger of being deceived by Satan's lies. One person in isolation is easy to entrap. Two can resist. Three working together is extremely difficult for the enemy to effectively penetrate.

On her own, Kimberly was unable to see the lies. Though she knew God's promise to never leave or forsake us (Hebrews 13:5), when she tried to handle this particular situation on her own, she remained ensnared in Satan's web of lies. In isolation, she was deceived. She felt abandoned by God and saw no way forward.

But as we talked through this together, God began to open her eyes and show her the truth. Jesus was with her and never left her. She began to see how she was pushing Jesus away by believing the lie that she had committed an unforgivable sin. As we processed this new information together, she chose to reject these lies and instead trust Jesus' promises. Kimberly was able to accept Jesus' forgiveness by handing this box over to him and then forgiving herself. She felt the weight of this burden go and experienced peace around this situation for the first time in many years.

God wants us to use wisdom as we choose the people we bring into our inner circle. Not everyone is trustworthy. Not everyone has the maturity to keep your personal situation confidential. It is important to keep this circle small and prayerfully select the people with whom we share our burdens. When you feel like you are stuck and cannot find a way forward, it is important for this circle to be bigger than only God and you. It is important to include brothers or sisters in Christ who will walk alongside you and help you see the way forward.

18

repairing relationships

WHEN I WAS IN COLLEGE, a good friend of mine was smitten with the girl of his dreams. The two of them are happily married now, but in these early stages of the relationship, he was trying to win her heart. My buddy and I had many late-night discussions about the relationship. He would recount every casual encounter and replay each conversation, trying to find a way to win her heart.

"Did I say the right thing?"

"Was I acting stupid?"

"I hope I didn't turn her off!"

One night, I wanted to help my buddy get off this emotional roller-coaster, so I said, "I don't think you need to worry so much. People are not so fragile!"

After a moment of thought, he made a statement which has stuck with me ever since, "Maybe not, but relationships are!"

Relationships are one of God's greatest blessings. We were created to desire friendship and connection. When our relationships are healthy, life is good, but even the strongest relationships can be damaged or destroyed when handled carelessly. It is important for us to take care and seek God's wisdom as we determine how to move forward in our relationships.

In his second letter to the church in Corinth, Paul deals with some difficult, moral situations which arose within their church body. These situations caused conflict and pain. But as he wraps up this letter, he includes the following words: "Finally, brothers and sisters, rejoice! Strive for full restoration, encourage one another, be of one mind, live in peace. And the God of love and peace will be with you" (2 Corinthians 13:11).

When relationships are damaged and broken, God desires for these relationships to be restored. Relationships are important to us, and they are important to God. He cares about friendships, families, and marriages. He wants these relationships to succeed. This is not only honoring to God, but it brings peace and joy to us as well. So—when we practice forgiveness—the ultimate goal is often reconciliation. When we choose to forgive ourselves for mistreating another person, often the next step is to work towards reconciliation with this person.

IF IT IS POSSIBLE...

The writer of the letter to the church in Romans writes these words: "If it is possible, as far as it depends on you, live at peace with everyone" (Romans 12:18).

In most situations, reconciliation is the right goal and worth working toward. Reconciliation feels good. It seems right—like the final step. However, reconciliation requires two willing parties. As a result, sometimes reconciliation is not possible. Though we may truly desire it, it's not always a realistic outcome. In fact, we know it's not always *wise* to attempt to reconcile with every offender, even though we have forgiven them.

As we look at the Gospels, we can't help but notice: Jesus himself was not able to reconcile with everyone. When he was here on earth, he loved everyone with a perfect love. But it is well known how the religious elite hated Jesus (John 11:53, Matthew 12:14, Mark 3:6). The people in his own neighborhood took offense with him (Mark 6:3). Even Judas, one of his own disciples who lived with him for three years, ultimately rejected him (Luke 22:48, Matthew 27:5). When Jesus walked the earth, he wanted to live at peace with everyone. We know he was God's Son and always treated people in a godly way. But because it takes two people to reconcile a relationship, even Jesus himself was unable to live at peace with everyone! God knows reconciliation is not always possible even if we faithfully do our part.

> reconciliation is a good goal, but not always a realistic outcome

In this chapter, I want to unpack some principles I hope will be helpful in deciding how to proceed in each relationship after completing the forgiveness process. Is reconciliation a good idea in this situation? Will it be helpful or hurtful? Now that I have forgiven, how should my relationship with this person change?

Before we start, though, it is important to be reminded that forgiveness is a transaction between God and you. When you practice biblical forgiveness, your relationship with God is immediately restored. Regardless of whether you are able to reconcile with any other person in the situation, you can be confident forgiveness has done its full work and we are, most importantly, reconciled in our relationship with God!

PRINCIPLE #1:
FORGIVE FIRST

Janet was so full of contradicting emotions that she didn't know what to do next. She agreed to take a new job working for her cousin; it did not go well. A few weeks into the job, the relationship was quickly souring. After being confronted for a minor infraction, Janet and her cousin got into an argument. It became so heated that she could not remember whether she quit or was fired. But she found herself jobless, carrying not only shame for the way she acted, but also resentment towards her cousin.

> when we feel God is leading us to reconcile, it is important to forgive first

Janet wanted to resolve the situation with integrity but was struggling to find a way forward. Because I was outside of the situation, it was easier to see how the fog of bitterness had affected her judgment. As we talked, Janet began to list all the "things that needed to be said" to her cousin.

I suggested to Janet, "Before you call or send any emails, it may be helpful to forgive her. Would you be willing to do this?"

Janet reluctantly agreed, and we worked through the forgiveness process. She chose to forgive her cousin and also forgave herself for her part in the situation. Janet felt the burden of bitterness go as Jesus took it and immediately replaced it with his peace.

When she finished the forgiveness process, I encouraged her, "Now, why don't you ask Jesus what you should communicate to your cousin."

She was silent as she prayed. After a short time, her face showed a look of surprise. "Oh," she said aloud.

Curious about her reaction, I asked, "Did God give you any direction?"

She said with a quiet confidence, "I thought there were things that 'needed to be said.' I'm not sure anything else needs to be said at all!"

In the fog of bitterness, our judgment is impaired. Because unforgiveness damages our relationship with God, it is more difficult to hear his voice of wisdom. For this reason, it is important to forgive before we decide if and how to move toward reconciliation.

Once Janet forgave her cousin, God gave her the wisdom she needed. When the bitterness dissipated, she saw more clearly how to move forward in a way which would give grace to her cousin and bring healing to the entire family. It was not an easy road forward, but God gave Janet the grace to work toward reconciliation.

When we feel God is leading us to approach the other person, it is so important to forgive first. We don't need the other person's consent to forgive. By releasing the unforgiveness, we restore our relationship with God. This enables us to be equipped with the fruit of the Spirit if we choose to approach the person. Though we can never guarantee how the other person will respond, forgiveness will free us to enter the conversation with a spirit of love, joy, peace, patience, kindness, goodness, faithfulness, gentleness, and self-control (Galatians 5:22-23).

It is important to remember the purpose of this kind of communication is *restoration*. The purpose is not to make sure the offender understands "how much they have hurt us," nor is it to "make sure they never do this again." These are matters of justice. When we forgive, we are putting the matter of justice into Jesus' hands. The purpose of this communication is to attempt to restore a relationship in a healthy way. Of course, we hope the offender will respond in a way which allows us to begin—over time—to rebuild a relationship of trust. God is responsible for these kinds of ultimate outcomes. He holds each of us responsible for our own actions. Once we forgive the offender, we need not take back any responsibility for how the person responds to our attempt to reconcile the relationship.

PRINCIPLE #2:
KEEP SAFE BOUNDARIES

Christina's mother was extremely self-centered. Though her mother typically had good intentions, her words were often very hurtful. Christina's mother was easily offended but seemed completely unaware of how offensive and hurtful her own words were to others. Christina's children were now old enough to be aware of grandma's harsh tone and often came away feeling wounded themselves. Visits with her mother were becoming more and more upsetting to the entire family. Whenever Christina tried to confront her mother, she would become indignant and tell Christina she was being "too sensitive" and needed to "lighten up."

As she sat in my office with her husband, Christina tearfully said to me, "I don't think I can forgive my mother anymore."

"Why not?" I asked her.

"Because I can't continue to put my family through these awful visits. It takes our family almost a week to get over all the emotions she stirs up," she said.

"Why do you think God wants you to keep tolerating this kind of hurtful behavior?" I asked.

"Well, if I truly forgive my mother, won't we need to spend time with her? Won't we need to be reconciled?" she asked.

God desires for us to live at peace with everyone, but does this mean God expects us to willingly put ourselves (or those in our care) back into harm's way? Of course not. Once we complete the forgiveness process, it is important for us to establish healthy boundaries to protect us (and our loved ones) from further injury. God has given us the responsibility to protect those in our care. Forgiveness does not mean we need to restore trust. Often the offenses, though forgiven, demonstrate why the offender is not trustworthy.

> if there is no prior relationship, there is no relationship to be reconciled.

God wants us to use wisdom. It is appropriate and necessary to put boundaries in place to protect ourselves and others from being hurt again. Our hope is for the offender to change and earn back our trust but putting boundaries in place will protect us from further harm. If the offender has changed, then trust can be earned again over time.

Dr. Henry Cloud and Dr. John Townsend have written a fantastic series of books on this subject, the first one titled, *Boundaries: When to Say Yes, How to Say No to Take Control of Your Life*. If creating boundaries in your relationship is an area of struggle for you, I would encourage you to check out this series. It is a reading which has been very helpful in forming my own understanding of healthy boundaries.

Christina and her husband decided it would be wise to have this difficult conversation with her mother without the kids present. She explained to her mother how her words were hurtful, damaging, and unacceptable. They set some hard boundaries with her and plainly laid out which topics of conversation were no longer acceptable. As a couple, they chose to limit the length of time the kids would spend with grandma when they visited.

Christina's mother never acknowledged any responsibility for hurting Christina or her kids. Christina and her husband continued to enforce their new boundaries anyway. This was all very painful for Christina's mother, but she began to realize—if she wanted to spend time with her grandchildren—she had to respect those boundaries.

Christina did forgive her mother. And with this biblical understanding of forgiveness, she knew she was doing the right thing. She felt empowered to protect herself and her children by putting healthy boundaries in place.

PRINCIPLE #3:
STRANGERS MAY REMAIN STRANGERS

Devan was mugged at knifepoint. The criminal was caught and went to jail. Though the man was incarcerated and paying for his crime, the traumatic experience left Devan very upset. He decided to forgive the criminal and completed the forgiveness process. Although Devan felt a newfound sense of freedom, he still had some nagging questions. "I feel like I should visit this criminal in jail or something," he told me.

"Visiting this man sounds awful to me, but if I have really forgiven him—shouldn't I reach out to tell him I have forgiven him?"

"Did you know the man before he attacked you?" I asked.

"No," Devan replied.

"So—because he attacked you—this means now you have a responsibility to enter into a relationship with him?" I challenged.

We have all heard wonderful stories about how godly men and women have forgiven violent offenses and—by the grace of God—have miraculously developed friendships with the perpetrator. These are the amazing stories that make the news. In some rare cases, God may ask us to do this, but these stories are the exception, not the rule.

As a general principle, when an offense is committed against us by another person we have little or no relationship with, it is not necessary for us to initiate a new relationship through a reconciliation process. *Reconciliation* is the restoration of a relationship. If there is no prior relationship, there is no relationship to be restored. Forgiveness means we are placing both the offenses and the offenders in God's hands. We can feel free to leave the offenses and the offender with God and move forward with our own lives.

PRINCIPLE #4:
DO NOT PUT YOURSELF IN HARM'S WAY

Valerie's father was an alcoholic and physically abusive. When she went off to college, her life got a lot easier and a lot better. While in college, at age nineteen, she decided to forgive her father. Valerie wondered if she should attempt to confront her father about his abuse. Like any daughter, she cared about her father and was hopeful she could begin to restore the relationship by getting it all out in the open.

I asked her, "How would you expect your father to react if you confronted him about his abusive behavior?"

"I hope he would feel sorry. I hope he would ask for my forgiveness," she said introspectively.

"I *hope* he would, too," I answered, "but have you ever confronted him in the past? How did he respond?"

"I guess I did one time. He was furious and started stomping around the house and yelling. It really scared me," she said.

"I know you want to have a healthy relationship with your father," I said, "but it might not be safe to confront him in this way."

In some cases, it simply may not be safe to attempt to reconcile with another person. In other cases, it may be helpful and wise to consider the circumstances or location of this kind of meeting. Perhaps the meeting should take place in a more public environment or even with a third person to ensure your safety.

> those who are wise will seek out and listen to advice from trustworthy people

When offenses rise to the level of violence or abuse, it is completely appropriate to terminate the relationship. It may be necessary to involve government authorities to help put an end to the abusive behavior. These kinds of boundaries may seem extreme, especially when the offender is a family member or someone close. We become an enabler when we continue a relationship which will almost certainly result in more abuse and pain. It is not only for our own protection, but also to help ensure others are not hurt by this person in the future.

The important principle is that we should not unwisely put

ourselves or other people in harm's way as we attempt to restore a broken relationship. There are circumstances when it is not reasonable to approach the offender or attempt to restore a relationship. In these situations, reconciliation may be impossible and unwise.

PRINCIPLE #5:
DO NOT DAMAGE THE OTHER PERSON

When Ned was a teenager, he was in an extended relationship with a classmate and crossed some of her moral boundaries. Ned came to me because he felt the Holy Spirit was prompting him to deal with these sins. Though Ned didn't fully comprehend the gravity of these choices as a teenager, he now understood his actions could have caused a lasting, negative impact on his high school girlfriend.

All these years later, Ned still felt guilty about the way he treated her. We walked through a process of confession and self-forgiveness. Ned put each of his offenses in a box and gave it all to Jesus. When he finished, Ned said to me, "I don't know where she is now, but these events may still be affecting her. I wonder if I should find her and ask for her forgiveness, too. If she is struggling with this in any way, perhaps this would help give closure."

After some thought, I responded to Ned, "I know your heart is in the right place, but I am not sure this would be wise or helpful. You have not seen or talked to her for over twenty years. We don't know how this is affecting her today. She may have already forgiven you and moved on with her life. She may be happily married and have a wonderful relationship with her husband. She may not remember it at all. If you approach her now, you may cause her more pain. We don't know."

Ned and I prayed together, seeking God's wisdom, and both felt it would not be helpful to seek out and approach this woman. Instead, God encouraged Ned to pray for her any time the Holy Spirit brought this situation back into his mind. Ned was encouraged when he saw how he could have a positive impact through prayer.

When we consider how we approach others who are involved in these situations, it is important we avoid causing damage to the person. Perhaps the person is not aware of the offense. If our goal is reconciliation, it may not be necessary or helpful to point out every minor offense. A well-meaning attempt to "reconcile" the relationship may instead stir up more conflict and further damage the relationship. In many situations, working through the forgiveness process with Jesus may be enough to restore the relationship.

When it comes to relationships, "good intentions" are not a sufficient excuse for any course of action. Even the best intentions can result in hurt and more brokenness. It is critical to take a step back and consider whether our words and actions will bring healing.

PRINCIPLE #6:
SEEK WISE COUNSEL

It is extremely helpful and wise to seek the advice of trustworthy brothers or sisters in Christ. Relationships are built on trust, and we may need an outside perspective to ensure that we do not inadvertently damage this trust. When we rely only on our own intuition, we can unintentionally harm ourselves, those in our care, or even the person with whom we are attempting to reconcile.

If we are in doubt regarding the best way to proceed . . . If our attempts to reconcile have not gone well in the past . . . If we are worried about the outcomes and consequences of attempting to restore a relationship, it is important for us to approach trustworthy brothers or sisters in Christ who can help us find the best path forward.

We may be confident our approach is "right." But getting another perspective from someone who is outside the situation is still important. Remember Solomon's words:

"The way of fools seems right to them, but the wise listen to advice" (Proverbs 12:15).

"Plans fail for lack of counsel, but with many advisers they succeed" (Proverbs 15:22).

Those who are wise will seek out and listen to advice from trustworthy people. A few inappropriate words can be extremely destructive to even the strongest relationships (James 3:3-12). In each of the principles in this chapter, seeking out wise counsel can help us avoid pitfalls which bring damage to ourselves and to others. Of course, we need to make our own choices in the end, but when we hear and honestly consider the advice of others, it often helps us proceed in a way that is more likely to bring peace and joy and healing to all involved in the situation.

APPLYING THE PRINCIPLES

After completing the forgiveness process, we must consider how to proceed with relationships. It's important to remember, though, none of these principles of reconciliation should be taken as absolutes to be blindly applied to every situation. Each person is unique, and every situation must be prayerfully assessed. We need to be willing to follow the leading of the Holy Spirit as we consider the best way forward in each relationship.

The good news is that God gladly provides wisdom when we ask (James 1:5-8)! He has given each of us individual gifts, because it is his plan for us to be dependent upon one another within the Body of Christ (1 Corinthians 12). It is important to approach trustworthy men and women who have gifts of discernment and wisdom. We should listen to their advice as we consider the best path forward in each relationship and in each situation.

19

forgiveness and traumatic events

"I WAS ON THE PHONE with my sister, and we got in an argument. She said some hurtful things."

"My good friend was murdered during a robbery."

These are both examples of offenses which require forgiveness. But it does not take a doctorate in psychology to realize that the scale of the impact of each situation will be very different. When we are dealing with traumatic events or offenses, there are some considerations we must keep in mind as we go through the forgiveness process and seek God's release from the burden of carrying resentment.

GOD'S POWER IS SUFFICIENT

Here is the good news. There are no additional steps in the forgiveness process for more severe offenses. The process is the same, and we can follow the same checklist. God's power to take responsibility for an offense is not dependent on its severity or weight. It does not matter how big the offense seems to us or how large a box we need to put it in. God is able to handle it! It is never too big for him, and he is always ready to take them from us.

I have found it's important to address some additional areas where people get stuck even though they complete a process of forgiveness.

"Why am I still so sad? I thought if I forgave, I would be totally free."

"I forgave the drunk driver, so why did I get so angry on my daughter's birthday?"

"How could God allow our baby to die alone in his crib? God could have prevented this! How could he let this happen?"

These are the types of questions we are faced with when we have to deal with the fallout of some of the heaviest tragedies of life. Life on this earth is not easy! Often, well-meaning people give trite, religious answers. We all need to be very careful not to give the kind of advice which brings more shame or brokenness. Instead, there are some healing tools God has given that provide a way forward through these kinds of tragedies.

WHY AM I STILL SO SAD?

Matthew 5:4 says, "Blessed are those who mourn, for they will be comforted." Jesus gives us a simple yet profound truth: mourning is the way to comfort. Forgiveness does not take away all our emotions. Sadness is a healthy emotion, designed to let us know we have lost something important or someone dear to us. When we grieve our loss, Jesus promises we will find comfort.

In my son's sophomore year, a classmate died tragically and unexpectedly. This young man was loved by everyone, including students and teachers alike. The day after his death, a teacher and school counselor came into my son's history class to explain what happened. Everyone sat in shock. All they could do was stare at the floor. Many of the students were overwhelmed with emotion and began to cry. A few remained stoic, expressing no emotion.

As my son looked around the room, he first noticed the kids who outwardly showed sadness. Both students and teachers came around those students to comfort them. He noticed that the kids who showed no emotion were left to themselves; no one comforted them. Everyone assumed they did not need any help. It was a remarkable observation by my teenage son, demonstrating the truth of Jesus' proverb.

> it does not matter how big the offense seems to us God is able to handle it

This young man was so well-loved, over one thousand fellow students and several hundred adults came to his funeral. The family welcomed everyone who knew and loved their son to enter into the mourning process with them. The funeral was painful, but my son told me, "It was so much easier to go through it with other people."

Grief is real. Mourning is the path to comfort. Take time to remember what you have lost. You do not need to go through it alone. Yes, parts of this will be painful, and you will need to allow yourself to feel the difficult emotions. The mourning process takes time and personal investment. It is important to have a balance between finding time to care for yourself as well as support from others. We must enter into our grief to find the comfort and healing God promises.

WHY DO I STILL GET SO ANGRY?

Sheri's daughter was killed by a drunk driver. In my office, she worked through the forgiveness process. It was transformational, and she walked out with a new sense of freedom and joy.

As Sheri sat in my office six months later, she could not understand why her anger and outrage had returned. She was sure she had forgiven the drunk driver. She had given God responsibility, but Sheri was once again facing powerful feelings of anger and resentment. I asked her to explain what she was experiencing.

> it is important to be aware that new offenses can arise even after we have forgiven

Through her tears, Sheri said, "Last week would have been my daughter's eighteenth birthday. My daughter is gone, and the drunk driver is still alive. Her passage into adulthood should have been a joyous occasion, but he stole all this away from me. I know I have forgiven him, but I am so angry! I almost feel like the accident happened all over again. Why do I feel like this?"

In situations like this, the ongoing consequences of the initial event will often continue to create new offenses in the future. Often these new offenses are related to holidays or special events which can feel stolen away.

"I never got to see my daughter graduate."

"This would have been our twenty-fifth wedding anniversary."

"My ex-husband showed up at a family event with his new wife."

Though we may have forgiven everything we experienced in the past, it is important to recognize these situations as new offenses. We need not feel guilt or shame when these new offenses bubble up to the surface. We can simply bring these new offenses to God, so we can once again experience freedom and peace.

When we experience tragic and traumatic events, it is important to be aware that new offenses can arise even after we have forgiven the offender(s). God is faithful and ready to help us deal with these new offenses. We can put each offense into a box and Jesus will take them all away.

HOW COULD GOD LET THIS HAPPEN?

Leanne said, "My dad was a missionary. Why would God take him away from me? I was in middle school! My family says, 'I just need to trust God,' but God didn't save my dad. I had to grow up without a father. I loved my dad, and I needed him. How can I trust God after he did something so terrible?"

These are heart-wrenching questions. The Bible tells us God is good (Psalm 100:5), and God is just (2 Thessalonians 1:6). God only acts in ways which are consistent with his righteousness and goodness (1 John 1:5). But while we are in the middle of the hardest stuff of life, doesn't it seem reasonable to question God's goodness? Where did it go, we ask? Though directing her anger at God may not be based on good theology, it is certainly understandable in the midst of Leanne's pain.

Some well-meaning people toss around religious slogans. We hear statements like, "You just need to trust Jesus," or "You know, God works all things for our good." While these statements are theologically correct, hearing them makes us feel more confused and alone in our hurt. To Leanne, it seemed like her family was trying to convince her that her father's death was an act of God's goodness. What was good about her father dying? Growing up without her dad wasn't good, and it certainly wasn't fair!

When we are suffering from the pain of a traumatic experience or terrible loss, we may begin to question God's goodness. It is understandable for us to wonder if we can ever trust God again. Even the most closely held beliefs in God and his character can be challenged when we are experiencing this level of personal and emotional pain.

Jesus is not surprised or shocked by these kinds of questions. He is ready and waiting to walk through our pain—even our unbelief—with us. Though our faith may be shaken, God is a loving father who will gladly walk alongside us and help to carry these burdens (Matthew 11:28-29). Though we may choose to push God away from us, he will never push us away. Even when our anger and resentment are directed at God himself—it will not separate us from God's loving care (Romans 8:35-39).

So how can we deal with feelings of anger and resentment towards God? How do I approach God when I am not sure I can trust him? The answer to these questions is actually quite simple and straightforward. Like with the forgiveness process, we can simply put our anger and resentment in a box and give it to Jesus. He will take each box and the hurt and resentment it contains.

I have walked through these kinds of dark places with men and women as they approach Jesus openly and honestly. I can tell you with confidence: God is loving and faithful even in these situations. He wants his children to approach him for help even when we feel resentment toward him. He is waiting for his kids to come to him. He wants to have a transparent and authentic relationship with us. He doesn't want us to act like we still trust him when we do not. He does not expect us to "buck up" and pretend we fully trust when our faith is shaken to its core. This kind of pretending is counter-productive and hinders an authentic relationship with God.

God is our loving Father, and we have the freedom to tell him exactly what is bothering us. Jesus already knows our minds and our hearts. He will not be shocked or offended if we explain to him the reasons we are angry with God. He understands our hurt, our confusion, and our emotions. As we explain to Jesus, we can put each item in a box. When the box is full, we can pick it up and hand it to him. He will gladly take the hurt and the resentment away from us.

> even when our anger and resentment are directed at God himself—it will not separate us from God's loving care

I encouraged Leanne to follow the steps in the chart included at the end of this chapter. I said, "Be open and honest as you tell Jesus about the hurt you feel. Tell Jesus about the resentment you hold toward God. He already knows how you feel. You are simply telling him what he already knows."

In the quiet of her mind, Leanne stood in Jesus' presence. At first, she couldn't trust him enough to look at him. But through her tears, she began to explain to Jesus the ways she felt like God had cheated her out of the years she missed with her dad. She explained to Jesus how hurt she was because her father would never walk her down the aisle when she got married. One by one, she told Jesus about each item on her list. Though it was difficult at first, she chose to put each anger, hurt, and resentment in her box as she explained it to Jesus.

Leanne sealed up the box. As she tried to lift it, the box was too heavy. I noticed a surprised look on her face. "What happened?" I asked.

She told me through her tears, "When I couldn't lift the box, Jesus came over and helped me to pick it up. It was too heavy for me to lift on my own, but it did not seem very heavy to Jesus. He helped me pick it up, and he took it away."

I watched as Leanne settled into her chair. The tension seemed to drain out of her. "I feel like a huge weight has been lifted from my shoulders," she said with tears still in her eyes. She paused to thank Jesus for taking these burdens from her.

For Leanne, giving her resentment to God was an important step in restoring the joy which had been stolen from her for many years. Slowly, she began to trust God again. As Leanne's relationship with God grew, she began to see how God had been with her throughout the entire journey. She was on her way to healing.

WHEN I FEEL ANGRY AT GOD

Meet with Jesus | In the quiet of your heart and mind, notice that you are in a favorite place and Jesus is with you.

1. state the reasons you are angry with God

Tell Jesus how you believe God has hurt you and how this has affected you. | Remember you are the prosecuting attorney, not the defense attorney. God already knows how you feel. He will not be shocked or offended. He wants you to be open and honest with him.

2. the box

Notice there is a box next to you | Most people choose a simple moving-size, cardboard box.

Place each hurt in a box | You may put everything in the same box or use multiple boxes if one seems too full.

3. giving the box to Jesus

Seal the box shut

Pick up each box and feel the weight of the full box | If the box is too heavy, ask Jesus to help you pick it up.

Give each box to Jesus | As you give the box to Jesus, tell him you are giving him responsibility for the things in the box. Feel the weight of it go as he takes it away. Everything in the box is now his.

Ask Jesus if there are any other ways you believe God has hurt or failed you | Ask and notice what offenses come to mind.

For any additional hurts or resentments brought to mind, start again with "step 1. state the reasons you are angry with God" | Continue to repeat steps 1 through 3 until no other hurts or resentments come to mind.

Don't get discouraged if God brings many things to mind and you need to repeat these steps several times. God wants you to be free. He wants to restore his relationship with you.

4. thankfulness

Thank Jesus | Thank Jesus for making a way to be free from these hurts and resentments through his death on the cross. Thank him for giving you this freedom.

GOD'S GRACE IN TRAGEDY

We live in a fallen world (Romans 5:12). Tragedy is all around us. When we are caught in the backwash of these kinds of awful events, it can feel overwhelming. The emotional strategies and spiritual tools we have used for dealing with difficult times in the past may fall short in the face of this level of pain and turmoil. The negative emotions can come at us in waves and feel inescapable. It may even cause us to doubt our faith.

It is important for us to be aware when we are faced with these kinds of trials. We need other brothers and sisters in Christ to support us and give us wisdom. Mourning is often the path to finding comfort. When new offenses arise and bring a new wave of anger or resentment, we don't need to be surprised. This is normal. We can forgive these new offenses and continue to live in freedom.

Even if our faith is shaken to its core, and we become angry at God, he does not push us away. He is a loving Father who will patiently hear our complaints. When these experiences create barriers in our relationship with God, Jesus is able to remove these and trust can be restored.

20

keeping short accounts

IT WAS A FAIRLY NORMAL DAY, except for one thing. I kept getting angry at people. Not anyone in particular, but random people from my past. I felt like there was a commercial interruption popping up in my mind every few minutes highlighting another memory of someone I was still angry with. The events were small: insults, manipulation, mistreatment, or unfairness. Even so, the anger kept bubbling up in my mind.

God was teaching me about the principles of forgiveness, and I was learning to apply them in my own life. I practiced recognizing these feelings of anger and bitterness, no matter how "mild" they seemed to me. I was training myself to immediately bring these offenses to Jesus and forgive. So, each time a new memory presented itself, and I felt the associated anger or resentment, I walked through the forgiveness process with Jesus. Each time he was faithful, each time he took another box from me, and each time he took the weight of the offenses away. I must have repeated the process at least a dozen times on this particular day. I was exhausted.

At some point, early in the afternoon, I was trying to work when another memory came to the surface. By now, I was irritated. I was tired of the emotional rollercoaster—feeling the full weight of the offense and then the release of giving it to Jesus. Besides, I needed to get some work done!

In spite of my annoyance, I came to Jesus in prayer and put the offense in the box. But before I handed him the box, I decided to be transparent with him about my irritation. I prayed, "How many people am I going to have to forgive today?"

Perhaps you can guess the Bible story God immediately brought to mind?

> 21Then Peter came to Jesus and asked, "Lord, how many times shall I forgive my brother or sister who sins against me? Up to seven times?" 22Jesus answered, "I tell you, not seven times, but seventy-seven times" (Matthew 18:21-22).

SEVENTY TIMES SEVEN

When I was a young child, I remember reading this passage. In the New American Standard Bible, the passage was translated "seventy times seven." I couldn't do this kind of math in my head, but I knew it was a very large number. I imagined a bully punching me over and over. *A good Christian would forgive the bully every time,* I thought. I was fairly certain that I had a limit. I didn't think I could ever live up to this lofty standard Jesus put before his disciples.

So, when this verse came to mind sitting at my desk that afternoon, it did not alleviate my frustration. I still knew I could never measure up to God's seventy-times-seven standard. My response was short and pointed, "Seriously?"

But immediately after I expressed my frustration, in my mind, I saw Jesus' response. He gave me a quiet and compassionate smile. No judgement, only understanding. Then I heard him say, "Well, I guess you could keep hanging on to all this resentment."

I melted.

Because in that moment, I felt like God's Spirit explained a principle of forgiveness I never understood before. I always thought the seventy-times-seven principle was a command to achieve God's high standard of goodness and compassion towards others. But I believe the reason the Holy Spirit kept bringing these memories to my mind was different. God wanted me to be free from them. He wanted me to find a peace which would otherwise remain out of reach.

> a lifestyle of forgiveness is a lifestyle of freedom

Jesus wants us to be free and to *live* free. He gave us the seventy-times-seven principle so we can be unshackled from the burdens which weigh us down.

FORGIVENESS AS A LIFESTYLE

A lifestyle of forgiveness is a lifestyle of freedom. Jesus died to give us unrestricted access to his forgiving power. God does not want us to have to carry these burdens. I have learned to keep short accounts. When people offend me, and I notice the offense continues to affect me, I bring these to Jesus quickly and do not let them fester in my heart and mind. Remember, this isn't letting the person off the hook. It's putting the offender on Jesus' hook and trusting that he will make things right.

Forgiveness can, over time, become part of the rhythm of our lives. When we first begin to practice forgiveness, the process may feel slow and awkward, but over time, practicing a process of forgiveness will become more natural and take less time. Of course, we may still have doubts at times. It may be difficult to trust God and release some offenses into his care which seem "too big" or "too awful," but even in the midst of the doubts, we can learn to trust Jesus with our boxes and give thanks as he takes each one. Over time, the process will become a practiced, go-to response, and unforgiveness will not creep into our hearts any longer. Forgiveness will become a natural part of living out our relationship with God. Freedom!

acknowledgements

We both would like to say how much we appreciate our wives and our children: Mary Snuffer and kids—Katherine, Zachary, Adrian, and Josiah, and Doreen Henderson and kids—Michael and K.D. Our families are partners in our ministry. They contributed to this project in numerous ways and supported us through the long hours spent working on this book.

We appreciate our partners at Good Soil Press who recognized the value in this work, provided a wealth of knowledge and expertise, and skillfully coached us through the process of publishing *Forgiveness: A Surprising Way Forward*.

—Michael Snuffer and Mark Henderson

in memory of
mark henderson

MARK DAVID HENDERSON, co-author of this book, passed away from cancer as this book was being finalized. Mark was a loving husband, father, and friend. He touched lives all over the world through his counseling ministry and often said he had a front row seat to God's miracles. He always made sure the individual knew it was God's healing, and Mark was simply the servant. His desire was to take what he learned and share it with others, which is the reason for this book.

A SPECIAL THANK YOU

After Mark Henderson's passing, our good friend and Mark's wife, Doreen, stepped up in a big way. Although Mark saw the manuscript to completion, Doreen helped me carry the book across the publishing finish line, and I'm very grateful. She worked diligently with our publisher's edit and design team at Good Soil Press to bring reader perspective and fine-tune the final product. Doreen was a great partner, reviewing all aspects of the book from her own perspective as well as representing Mark's viewpoint. Thanks for running the last lap with me, Doreen.

—Michael Snuffer

about the authors

Mark Henderson completed a Master's in Clinical Pastoral Counseling, and served as a pastor of counseling for twenty years. Michael Snuffer has ministered as a counselor for more than ten years. Mark and Mike founded Equip2Counsel™, a ministry dedicated to providing simple yet powerful counseling tools to ministers across the globe.

CPSIA information can be obtained
at www.ICGtesting.com
Printed in the USA
JSHW071035160423
40385JS00001B/1